VENICE
The Most Triumphant City

Marco Polo's Venice, 1338

VENICE
The Most Triumphant City

by

GEORGE BULL

NEW YORK
ST MARTIN'S PRESS

Copyright © 1981 by The Folio Society 1981
For information, write: St. Martin's Press,
175 Fifth Avenue, New York, N.Y. 10010
Printed in Great Britain

Library of Congress Catalog Card Number: 81-48328
ISBN 0-312-83864-6

First Edition

Contents

Acknowledgements

We would like to thank the following publishers and agents for permission to quote passages from published works in copyright: Mrs Eileen Scott-Moncrieff and Chatto & Windus Ltd for passages from *La Recherche du Temps Perdu* by Proust, translated by Scott-Moncrieff; W. H. Allen & Co Ltd for passages from *Palazzo* by Hans Habe; Laurence Pollinger Ltd and the estate of the late John Cowper Powys for a passage from his *Autobiography*, Hodder and Stoughton Ltd for a passage from *The Pleasant Years* by Cecil Roberts; Secker and Warburg Ltd for an extract from *Death in Venice* by Thomas Mann, translated by H. T. Lowe-Porter, and appearing in the publisher's edition, *Stories of a Lifetime*, Volume II, and The Bodley Head Ltd for an extract from *Eustace and Hilda* by L. P. Hartley.

Illustrations

8

Introduction

An apology for writing yet another book on Venice, in my case, would have to turn into a sort of *apologia pro vita sua*. This is a very personal book, rather more revealing about myself than I thought it would be when I first set out to write it, in the way that what people tell you about their taste in novels (as I know well) reveals their attitudes to life and their experience of it. In a sense, in contrast to books I have translated, edited, or constructed chiefly as a reporter, this is a first volume of autobiography.

And it is also another book on Venice, for my knowledge of which I have to thank the dead, whose works I pillage in the following pages, and the living, whose brains I have picked over the years. Among them are Herbert Jones, printer and typographer, who has educated me in those matters and sought out books and references for me as well. Margaret Mann Phillips who, knowing all about Erasmus, read what I had to say about him with a sharp and kindly eye. And Professor John Hale, whose generosity to me as I wandered occasionally in and out of his scholar's territory has been unstinted.

John Letts asked me to undertake this book and encouraged me courteously and constructively while it was being written, and so to him I owe my chief thanks. For the rest, I have learned from all my friends during the past few years what excitement the mention of the name of Venice can cause and in Venice, observing the Venetians and their works, have come to realise that the present as well as the past justifies this.

Veronese's painting of the Battle of Lepanto

1 Images of Venice

A city out of time, Venice is perpetually recreated as a work of art through the eyes of the artist and the writer. It yields a profusion of images like a hall of mirrors reflecting simultaneously and separately the constantly changing interpretations of the events of its history and its contemporary significance. When I began to write this book I remembered that my own first oblique image of Venice must have come from a poem I learnt by heart at my Jesuit school, when I was about fourteen, during the years of World War II. This was G. K. Chesterton's *Lepanto*, a painting in words which imposes the spirit of romantic medievalism and the form of a ballad on the paradoxical combination of an act of the Crusades and the Counter-Reformation. In this view of the second half of the sixteenth century, Venice, Spain and the Papacy, in a decadent and divided Christendom, hold the gates against the deathly assault of Islam, whose ships 'have dashed the Adriatic round the Lion of the Sea' and 'veiled the plumèd lions on the galleys of St Mark . . .'

Lepanto first appeared in Chesterton's *Collected Poems* in 1927. There are scarcely any references to Venice in all his books, but like so many others he had once known the perplexity of trying to tell to a friend the sights and emotions of a first visit. In 1894 he went on holiday to Italy, and in one of his letters to Edmund Clerihew Bentley (the author of a classic among detective stories, *Trent's Last Case*) he wrote: 'Imagine a city, whose very slums are full of palaces, whose every other house wall has a battered fresco, or a gothic bas-relief; imagine a sky fretted with every kind of pinnacle from the great dome of the Salute to the gothic spires of the Ducal Palace and the downright arabesque oriental-ism of the minarets of St Mark's; and then imagine the whole flooded with a sea that seems only intended to reflect sunsets, and you still have no idea of the place I stopped in for more than forty-eight hours. . . .' The twenty-one-year-old Chesterton expressed the normal wonder of someone who sees Venice for the first time. He had the additional curiosity of a painter and it is a pity he wrote no more about the city, except in a much-anthologised poem to allude to its part in a fateful European battle.

At school, of course, there was Shakespeare as well as Chesterton for learning by heart, and there were intimations of Venice in his projections of the majesty of the law and the power of the State; in the metaphors of Othello, there was a sense of the presence of the sea, and of Europe in crisis: 'The Turk with a most mighty preparation makes for Cyprus.'

Partly, I imagine, through friendship with a half-Italian boy and his family, I left school with a fascination for Italy already formed, and finding myself serving as a surprised and perhaps surprising fusilier started to learn Italian. Then at Oxford I picked the Italian Renaissance as my 'special subject'. This encouraged writing and reading about Italy, and the set books offered inexhaustible emotional and intellectual supplies. They included Niccolò Machiavelli's *Il Principe*; Guicciardini's *Storia d'Italia*; Castiglione's *Il Libro del Cortegiano*; Giorgio Vasari's *Le Vite dei più Eccellenti Pittori*, and Luigi da Porto's *Lettere Storiche*. One was meant to read around the subject, and that brought in a catchment of sources from Dante to Cellini and of interpreters from Burckhardt onwards. In varying intensities, the form of historical Venice was reflected in these books. Machiavelli and Francesco Guicciardini, in sharp Tuscan prose, explained the envy, fear and suspicion of Venice that existed among other Italians, and not least the Florentines. Baldessar Castiglione, elegantly recounting the conversations that took place at the height of the Renaissance among the courtiers of Urbino, introduced the imposing figure of the revered Venetian humanist Pietro Bembo, whose neo-Platonic speech on the nature of Love concludes his influential book; but he also suggested the overshadowing of Venice, once so powerful, in the cultured and politically attuned minds of contemporary Italy by the power of Spain and France.

Vasari's *Lives* are flecked with lively and suggestive details of Venetian life and landscape. They communicate Vasari's delight in the work and success of the Bellini family, of Giorgione and especially Titian; but he praises the Venetians chiefly for their colouring, and sheds his strong light on the great Tuscan artists who triumph in the exaltation of Michelangelo. Less prejudiced impressions of war-stricken Renaissance Venice came from Luigi da Porto, who was born in the subject-town of Vicenza, fought for Venice in the war of the League of Cambrai and testified to the hold of Venice on the loyalties of the ordinary people of the mainland. Writing two hundred years before da Porto, Dante gave me my first sight – one might almost say touch and smell – of the stupendous Arsenal of Venice, when he used it as a metaphor to describe the place in the eighth circle of Hell where corrupt public officials are punished (a subject on which Dante felt strongly, having been accused himself of barratry).

> . . . *e vidila mirabilmente oscura.*
> *Quale nell'arzana de'Viniziani*
> *bolle l'inverno la tenace pece*
> *a rimpalmar li lor legni non sani,*
> *che navicar non ponno . . .*

> *Thus from bridge to bridge we came, with other*
>   *talk which my Comedy cares not to recite;*
>   *and held the summit, when*
> *we stood still to see the other cleft of Malebolge*
>   *and the other vain lamentings; and I found*
>   *it marvellously dark.*
> *As in the arsenal of the Venetians boils the*
>   *clammy pitch in winter; to caulk their*
>   *damaged ships,*
> *which they cannot navigate; and, instead*
>   *thereof, one builds his ship anew, one plugs the*
>   *ribs of that which hath made many voyages;*
> *some hammer at the prow, some at the stern;*
>   *some make oars, and some twist ropes; one*
>   *mends the jib, and one the mainsail:*
> *so, not by fire but by art divine, a dense pitch*
>   *boiled down there, and overglued the banks*
>   *on every side.* *

From Benvenuto Cellini I learned a lot about the seamy side, as well as the power and the glory, of Papal Rome, Medici Florence and royal Fontainebleau. He visited Venice in 1535 and 1546 where he met Sansovino and Titian, and the description in the *Life* of his journey to and from, by horse and boat, is a masterpiece of racy suspense. Burckhardt's solidly brilliant *Civilisation*

---

* *Inferno*: Eighth Circle. The Temple Classics translation.

of the Renaissance in Italy added to my so-far fragmentary knowledge of Venice the discernment of the Venetians' high-flown
and peculiar view of themselves as heirs of ancient Rome, almost
a chosen people. 'Venice recognised itself from the first as a
strange and mysterious creation – the fruit of a higher power than
human ingenuity . . .'

During my last year at Oxford in 1951, E. V. Rieu, a translator
of Homer and founder and first editor of the Penguin Classics, a
bold literary explorer, commissioned my first translation for the
series, the *Life* of Benvenuto Cellini, and so kept me firmly tied
to the study of the Italian Renaissance. Over the following
twenty years, I translated *The Book of the Courtier*, selected biog-
raphies from *The Lives of the Artists*, *The Prince* and some short
stories by Bandello; but Venice remained at the edge of my field
of vision, glimpsed through the eyes, chiefly, of Tuscans, Lom-
bards and Romans, but continuously creating its lasting impressions. I wondered about the visit there of Leonardo da Vinci (not
recorded by Vasari) in the year 1500 and imagined his offering
plans to the Signoria for military defence against the Turk; or
playing a lute made by his friend Lorenzo da Pavia, and staring at
the eddying waters of the Grand Canal.

In their imperial State on the lagoons, the Venetians, closer to
their fellow-Italians than the northern barbarians or the Turks,
nonetheless seemed a strange, almost alien people to other
Italians. This was partly a matter of Italian *campanilismo*, the
resilient local patriotism which can still arouse Italians to inflict
on each other extraordinary contempt and conflict. It also
reflected the divergent history of Italian states and cities, as
Stendhal noted in the nineteenth century when he recorded that
the simplest arts were carried out in totally different ways in
Italy's seven or eight centres of civilisation, of which Venice was
one. But the distinctiveness of Venice, the Venetians' historical
sense of destiny, transcends the common divisions of Italy and
casts its fascination over half the world. It is a physical as well as
an historical, an emotional as well as an intellectual, revelation,
this uniqueness of Venice.

After my own vivid but distanced images of Venice had been
formed in the ways I have described, I was asked in 1970 to
translate some of the writings of Pietro Aretino. I knew him
mostly for his reputation as a pornographer – author of the

Pietro Aretino by Titian

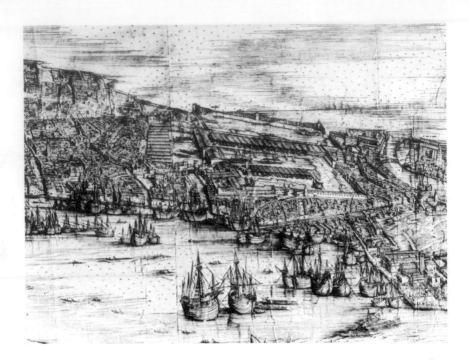

The Arsenal in the 16th century

sonnets which prompted Giulio Romano's paintings and Marcantonio Raimondi's engravings of the *Sedici modi* – and from references in Vasari to his friendship with Titian I began to read his plays, his verses, his letters. Suddenly, like a galleass whose broad decks were swarming with living figures, Venice seemed to loom for the first time into clear view. I could hear the creakings of the wood, feel the spray, taste the salt on my lips. Helped by the fact that Venice, the island rising from the high water, has changed so gradually since Aretino settled there, I felt, as I wrestled with the translation of letter after letter written over four centuries ago, that I was walking the rounds of the city with him in the flesh.

'Translating an autobiography', said John Addington Symonds (in the context of his own version of Cellini), 'enables the translator to get to know the subject *intus et in cute.*' Translating Aretino's letters and reading his other works brought me the feeling I knew intimately both the man painted so marvellously by Titian – with his heavy chain of gold from the King of France, thick, silky beard, sensual, sensitive, intelligent features, proud

San Marco in 1490

and heavy head – and, through his descriptions, the city and hinterland of the Venice he adopted, exploited and adored.

My discovery of Venice has continued through successive visits and, as it began, through a continuing voyage of literary exploration, noting the connections and contrasts between the historical realities, the ideas entertained by Venetians of themselves, and the images of Venice formed and communicated by visitors to the city since the golden and imperial age with its mid-point at the year 1500. Thus the form of this book is an anthology strung along a thread of historical narrative, interspersed by personal impressions and experiences. These have included a sharper awareness of the slight shift of interest among English-speaking academic scholars in the direction of Venice during the past few decades away from their traditional bias towards Florence. It has the bracing elements of rivalry noted by Professor John Hale in the Preface to the essays on *Renaissance Venice* edited by him and published in 1973, where he wrote that the book was planned 'in a mild spirit of partisanship' to complement Professor Rubinstein's *Florentine Studies* of 1968.

'. . . Fewer historians visit the archives of the Frari than those of Florence,' he noted, 'fewer still settle in Venice for the gestation of a major work.'

Perhaps English-speaking dons have neglected Venice in favour of Florence but not so, or far less so, have the writers and artists, otherwise there could be no book of this sort for me to write. Their successive love-affairs with Venice provide an *embarras de richesse* well illustrated, for example, by those who have written notable passages on the gondola alone: namely (according to Timothy Holme in his own entrancing *Gondola, Gondolier*) Shelley, Mark Twain, Goethe, George Sand, Thomas Mann, Byron, Hemingway, James Morris, Ernest Thorin, Richard Cobden, le Corbusier, and others. Standing on *his* balcony in Venice, James Morris reflected that the city was a kind of metropolis, in the sense that all the world came to visit her. 'Wherever I look', he said after scattering a handful of names from Byron and Ruskin to Beerbohm and d'Annunzio, 'I can fancy the shadows of famous men . . .'

My pursuit of images of Venice, and interrogation of the shadows of famous men, has also been stimulated by my having to return, from Venice itself or from reading about Venice, to the preoccupations of my professional life as a business journalist, and sometimes meditating on possible comparisons between the decline and survival of Venice and the decline and survival of Britain. If seriously pursued, the parallels vanish, but the affinities are real for those who love the two places, if you seek them in the sea, in response to music, in humour, in tolerance, in inventiveness, in the appetite for commerce, in aristocratic tradition, in the use by government of pageant, in the eye for profit, in the colonising instinct, in reverence for the State and a hundred other historical attitudes and experiences.

2 Light and Learning: the Renaissance

Julius II, the blunt warrior-Pope who told Michelangelo to make his statue with a sword in its hand, because he wouldn't know what to do with a book, could also wound with words. In a robust altercation with the Venetian ambassador, Giorgio Pisani, concerning Papal rights over Venetian benefices, he cried that he would know no rest till Venice were humbled and all Venetians were once again the fishermen they used to be.

The story is told in a letter of 1509 by Luigi da Porto, who suggests that Pisani rashly gave as good as he got and said that the Venetians would just as easily turn the Pope back into a raw little priest. The Pope's insult had a timeless quality, however. To call the Venetians fishermen was to suggest the insubstantial nature of their power and importance that might vanish just as the city might disappear like a dream beneath the waves. It echoes the first written description of the way of life of the early Venetians, which contains the faint promise of all the glory to come and the reminder of Venice's precarious physical existence between sea and sky.

The images are unforgettable once read and few writers on Venice can resist quoting them. Nor can I. The author was a sixth-century Calabrian, an influential scholar and founder of monasteries, a lover of sun-dials and water-clocks, who served the Ostrogothic kings of Italy, and was called Senator Flavius Magnus Aurelius Cassiodorus. Among the letters and edicts he published (under the title *Variae*) one from Ravenna dated the year 523 is addressed to the Emperor Theodoric's 'maritime tribunes' who are asked to make sure of the swift and speedy delivery along 'the pleasantest of rivers' of cargoes of wine and oil from Istria.

'For you live like sea birds, with your homes dispersed, like the Cyclades, across the surface of the water. The solidity of the earth on which they rest is secured only by osier and wattle; yet you do not hesitate to oppose so frail a bulwark to the wildness of the sea. Your people have one great wealth – the fish which suffices for

19

them all. Among you there is no difference between rich and poor; your food is the same, your houses are all alike. Envy, which rules the rest of the world, is unknown to you. All your energies are spent on your salt-fields; in them indeed lies your prosperity and your power to purchase these things which you have not. For though there may be men who have little need of gold, yet none there live who desire not salt.

'Be diligent, therefore, to repair your boats – which, like horses, you keep tied up at the doors of your dwellings . . .'

A thousand years after Cassiodorus lived, at the beginning of the sixteenth century, the Venetians seemed more exposed and vulnerable than ever they had been in their entire history (save perhaps once in war against Genoa). In a single day – at the battle of Agnadello, 14 May 1509 – was lost the land empire wrested from its neighbours by Venice during the previous hundred years.

After the French invaded Italy in 1494 (all their king had to do, wrote Machiavelli bitterly, was to mark where he wanted his billets – he won battles with a piece of chalk) alliances became unstable and the balance of Italian power was destroyed, and the Venetians, seizing the main chance wherever they saw it, had by 1508 provoked the formation against them of the ignoble alliance – the League of Cambrai – of the Pope and the Emperor, the kings of France, Aragon and Hungary, the rulers of Mantua and Ferrara. In the ensuing war, the 20,000-strong Venetian army – although an exceptionally powerful and capable-looking force for the Italy of the time – suffered from divided leadership and uncertain political command, and was routed twenty miles east of Milan. Few were killed but the mercenaries fled back towards the sea. One after the other, the subject-towns of Venice defected or were captured. In the city, frenzied preparations were made to withstand siege and assault.

A Venetian banker and chronicler, Girolamo Priuli, blamed the catastrophe on the degeneracy of the nobles and the sins of the people: delays in justice, slackness in nunneries, effeminacy in dress, sodomy and irreligion.

Just over ten years later in his *Florentine History*, Machiavelli brilliantly foreshortened the story of Venice to explain the lateness of its importance in the affairs of the Italian mainland; the

Niccolò Machiavelli

fatal consequence of its interventions. He dates the foundation of Venice from the middle of the fifth century.

'When Attila, the king of the Huns, was besieging Aquileia, the inhabitants, despairing, after many defeats, of their safety, took refuge as best they could with their moveables among the uninhabited sandbanks which stood at the head of the Adriatic sea.

'The Paduans, also, seeing the flames close to them, and fearing, now that Aquileia was destroyed, Attila would seek them out, carried all their most precious possessions down to the same sea, to a place called the Rivo Alto, whither they deported their women, children and old folk, retaining the young men in Padua for the defence of the city. Moreover the men of Monfelice and the inhabitants of the surrounding hills, actuated by the same fears, betook themselves to the sand dunes of the same sea. After the taking of Aquileia, and the sacking of Padua, Monfelice, Vicenza, and Verona, the Paduans and the stronger refugees still continued to inhabit the marshes that were around the Rivo Alto. Likewise all the people driven out by the same occurrences from the districts round about the town called in ancient times Venezia, had recourse to the same marshes. Thus, driven by necessity, they forsook their most lovely and fertile lands to live in a spot unfruitful, unsightly, and lacking all the conveniences of life.

'But the confluence of so many people at once made those places not only habitable but delightful, and they lived quite securely, founding among themselves laws and customs, and rapidly increasing in reputation and strength, whilst ruin and devastation was wrought in Italy.

'Moreover the Venetians, being compelled by force of circumstances to dwell in the midst of waters, were driven to devise some honest means of living independently of the land, and thus, faring with ships over the whole world, they filled their city with the merchandise which other men need, and for which men found it necessary to have recourse to Venice. For many years the Venetians desired no other dominion than that which would enable them to pursue their trade to the greatest advantage; they therefore acquired many ports in Greece and Syria, and for placing their fleets at the disposal of the French in the expeditions which they made into Asia, the island of Candia was granted to them as a reward.

'Whilst they lived in this way their name became dreaded at sea and respected within the confines of Italy. As time went on, the Venetians, impelled by the lust of dominion, seized Padua, Vicenza, Trevigi, and, later on, Verona, Brescia, and Bergamo, besides many cities in Romagna, and the kingdom of Naples, and their renown increased so greatly that not only to the princes of Italy but to the sovereigns beyond the Alps they became objects of fear.

'Hence a conspiracy was formed against them, and in one day they lost that dominion which with infinite pains they had built up during many years. Although in recent years they have regained some part of it, they have never recovered their former renown or power, and they live at the discretion of others, as do all other Italian principalities.'

In *The Prince* (written in 1513) Machiavelli blames the swift collapse of Venice in his time specifically on the employment of mercenary commanders. The mistakes of the Venetians were in forsaking their dominion over the sea for expansion on the land, and in failing to adapt their institutions to the times.

Doge Andrea Gritti

Doge Leonardo Loredano

The passage from Machiavelli's *Istorie Fiorentine* is of critical importance, both for the insight it gives into his mode of thought (being, as Burd mentions in his edition of *The Prince*, the *locus classicus* in his works on the subject of Venice), and for the way it reflects the ambiguous responses of contemporary Italy to the plight of Venice.

Set apart historically from the rest, republican in an age of despots, a haven for refugees, a place of beauty, dominant at sea, powerful, commercial and free, Venice was also envied, suspected and feared. The Italian rulers wanted Venice humbled but not crushed; Venetian possessions to fall into their laps, not into the alien hands of the French and the Germans.

Machiavelli never visited Venice, though his play, *Mandragola*, was performed there; but, during the war of the League of Cambrai, he was sent in 1509 to deal with the Emperor Maximilian and glean intelligence at Mantua and Verona, where he saw at first hand the way the tide of popular emotions was turning in favour of the Venetians in the areas where they had been dispossessed. 'The nobles do not love Venice, and incline to

23

the allies; but the people – the populace and the peasants – are all *Marcheschi.*'

During the French campaign against Venice, King Louis XII, son of a poet, had the peasants hanged who cried, '*Viva San Marco*'. He fought enthusiastically in the first rank at the battle of Agnadello which left the way clear for the French horsemen and foot-soldiers to move to the shores of the Venetian lagoon. The city might have been despoiled then as it was by another French conqueror, Napoleon, three hundred years later. The French took Cremona, Crema, Bergamo. Verona, Vicenza and Padua accepted the representatives of the Emperor. Venice's Neapolitan towns were restored to King Ferdinand, and the Pope's legate took possession of Rimini, Faenza, Cervia and Ravenna.

In Venice, sodomy may or may not have ceased, but, after Agnadello, recorded da Porto, many women altered their style of dress, the musicians who usually so delighted the inhabitants at that season as they played through the night were heard no more, and many talked of buying boats if they did not have them and fleeing the city, as Aeneas had fled Troy.

Fortunately, the Venetian decision to cede all that was asked, especially to the Emperor, halted the French armies and led to the withdrawal from the field of the French king, once he had been granted the possessions he claimed in the name of Milan.

From hindsight, the decision to release all Venetian subjects on the *terra firma* from their allegiance, and the promise that recriminations would not follow however matters progressed, looks more like cunning than cowardice, though it was certainly prompted by both. In any event, the French did not take Venice.

What treasures were there, they knew very well. The French crusaders had seen and left the memory of it. Geoffrey de Villehardouin, the Marshal of Champagne, embarked there on the Fourth Crusade which, in the early years of the thirteenth century, fastened the grip of Venice on the eastern Mediterranean for centuries to come.

Describing the negotiations of April 1201 between French envoys and the Venetian Council in the Doge's palace – 'a most beautiful building and very richly furnished' – Villehardouin puts vividly on to the page the earthy, enterprising shrewdness and business dignity of the Venetians as, through the Doge, they bargain with the knights over taking the cross.

'We will build transports to carry 4,500 horses and 9,000 squires, and other ships to accommodate 4,500 knights and 20,000 foot sergeants. We will also include in our contract a nine months' supply of rations for all these men and fodder for all the horses. This is what we will do for you, and no less, on condition you pay us five marks per horse and two marks per man . . .

'And we will do more than this. We will provide, for the love of God, fifty additional armed galleys, on condition that so long as our association lasts we shall have one half, and you the other half, of everything we win, by land or sea.'*

When the then Duke of Orleans, the future King Louis, rode with Charles VIII across the Alps into Italy, in 1494, so did the diplomat and writer, Philippe de Commynes, as far as Asti; then he parted with the royal army to negotiate with the Venetians while Louis stayed in the north and Charles progressed triumphantly to Pavia, Florence, Rome and Naples. Commynes remained for eight months in Venice, from October 1494 to May 1495. His task was to dissuade the Venetians from joining a league of Italian states against the French. He was not successful. He was present in July at the battle of Fornovo, fought near Parma when withdrawing French forces and the king were challenged by Italian mercenaries under the command of the Marquis of Mantua and two Venetian *proveditori*. The French got through; the Italians saved their camp; both sides claimed victory.

Commynes returned to Venice for fresh negotiations to persuade the Venetians to adhere to the Treaty of Vercelli (between Milan and France) which he had helped to negotiate. Again he failed. After his return to France, where he lost all influence on the death of Charles VIII, Commynes wrote the account of the king's expedition to Italy which constitutes the seventh and eighth book of his memoirs. In them is a Venice resplendent, seen through observant and appreciative eyes, near the turn of the century, when her reputation still holds as one of the great Italian city-states, even the dominant one, and as a power unmatched at sea.†

* From *Chronicles of the Crusades* trans. M. R. B. Shaw, Penguin Books 1963.
† Commynes was first translated into English by Thomas Danett, whose fourth, corrected edition of the *History* was published in 1596, dedicated to Lord Burghley. I quote from this rather than from the Victorian translation, Bohn's Standard Library, which I also have, by Andrew Scoble.

Politically, Commynes found the Venetians wise and well-governed, but 'inclined to enlarge their dominions' and therefore, he points out, a danger to their neighbours. When he expostulates about the league being formed, he is told by the Doge not to believe all he hears in town, 'for all men live there in liberty, and might speak what they liked.' He paints a conversation piece of the duke's council, as fresh and glowing as if newly done in oils:

'Then they sent for me again in a morning, and I found fifty or sixty of them assembled together in the Dukes Chamber, who lay sick of the Collick. He told me these news with a chearfull countenance, but none of the rest could dissemble so cunningly as himself: for some of them sate upon a low bench leaning upon their elbows, other some after one sort, and others after another; their outward countenances betraying their inward grief. And I think verily when word came to *Rome* of the battel lost at Cannae against *Hannibal*, that the Senators which remained in the City, were not more astonished nor troubled than these: for none of them once looked upon me, none of them gave me one word but the Duke alone; so that I wondered to behold them . . .'

This was after news had come of the fall to King Charles of the castle at Naples.

Commynes noted that there was no nation under the sun so suspicious as the Venetians nor so secret in their affairs 'so that sometimes they banish men upon suspicion only'. They were not as hardy or martial as the ancient Romans. They used mercenaries for war on the continent but their own nobility and subjects for the command and manning of expeditions at sea. They avoided civil contention; there were no popular tribunes; most of their people were 'strangers'.

The look of the city charmed and amazed him.

He had learned from the Duke of Milan before setting out for Venice that the Milanese ambassador had three gondolas to carry him about the town at no expense. 'Their ambassador hath the like at Milan, save that he hath no barge.' On the way, he passed by Brescia, Verona and Vicenza taking a boat down the Brenta from Padua, then noticing the little boats 'very proper and neat, covered with tapestry, and furnished within, with goodly hangings and velvet cushions to sit upon,' for the final lap to Venice.

Procession in the Piazza San Marco

After remarking the abundance of fish in waters that were usually calm, Commynes remembered:

'I wondered to behold the seat of this City, so many steeples, so many religious houses, and so much building, and all in the water; but especially that the people had none other passage to and fro in the Town but by boats, whereof I think there are to the number of 30000, but they be very small. Further, about the City (I mean within the compass round about of less than half a French league) are 70 houses of religion, as well of men as women, all in Islands, sumptuously built, richly furnished within, and having goodly gardens belonging to them. Those within the City I comprehend not in this number; for within, there are, besides these, the four orders of Friers, and threescore and twelve parishes, besides a number of chappels of the companies of occupations, commonly called Confrairies. And sure it is a strange sight to behold so many great and goodly Churches built in the Sea.'

Commynes' point of embarkation for Venice was Fusina, where Portia takes the ferry-boat from Belmont in *The Merchant of Venice*, and which, by the late nineteenth century, according to Augustus Hare, was 'only famous for its melons'.

He was met at Fusina by an escort of gentlemen and joined company with the ambassadors of Milan and Ferrara. Together

27

they visited the Church of Sant'Andrea, on the island; in magnificent boats holding about forty persons each they entered the Grand Canal – 'the great street, which is so large that the gallies pass to and fro through it, yea I have seen hard by the houses ships of four hundred tun and above.'

On the Grand Canal, Commynes reports that 'Their buildings are high and stately, and all of fine stone. The ancient houses be all painted, but the rest that have been built within these hundred years, have their front all of white marble, brought thither out of *Istria* an hundred miles thence and are beautified with many great pieces of Porphire and Serpentine. In the most part of them are at the least two chambers, the ceiling whereof is guilded, the mantletrees of the chimnies very rich, to wit, of graven marble, the bedsteds guilded, the presses painted and vermiled with gold, and marvellous well furnished with stuff. To be short, it is the most triumphant City that ever I saw.'

The next morning, Commynes presented himself to the Doge Agostino Barbarigo and admired the Palace, built of marble and fronted with stone gilt an inch thick, from where the Doge could pass to hear Mass at the high altar of the Chapel of St Mark's. This was 'the goodliest and richest Church in the world, bearing but the name of a chappel: for it is built throughout of the curious work called Musaique or Marquetery; the art also whereof they vaunt themselves to be authors of . . .'

The famous treasure included twelve or fourteen of the largest rubies Commynes ever saw, and twelve crowns of gold. 'Afterward they shewed me their other treasure, namely their Arsenal, where they arm their gallies, and prepare all other furniture necessary for their navy, which undoubtedly is the goodliest thing at this day in the world, and the best in order for that purpose.'

Among the next distinguished visitors to whom the Venetians showed off the Arsenal was Isabella d'Este, the most impressive of all the many remarkable women of the Italian Renaissance. She was the daughter of Duke Ercole of Ferrara (a frequent target for Venetian aggression), the sister-in-law of Elisabetta Gonzaga, depicted so warmly in Castiglione's *Book of the Courtier*, and the wife of Francesco Gonzaga, whom Castiglione served and who commanded the Italian forces at the battle of Fornovo in 1495. A discerning patron and correspondent of artists and a passionate, ruthless collector, painted by Titian, drawn by Leonardo da Vinci and praised by Ariosto, she loved Venice for its gaiety, for the books she ordered from the Aldine Press, for its Murano glass, for the friends she made there. Her first visit was in 1493 and she returned quite often, partly for pleasure, partly from diplomatic tact. Her experiences reveal all the charm and liveliness of the Venetian scene, sustained elegantly during years of war, defeat and recovery.

Isabella was nineteen, and three years married, when she first visited Venice at the invitation of the Doge, Agostino Barbarigo. She remarked on the rich jewellery of the ladies who attended her when she was received at Santa Croce, the sound of the bells, trumpets and guns as she was rowed up the Grand Canal, and the 'wearisome' nature of the ceremonies, including vespers in St Mark's and a state banquet. 'Have pity on me,' she wrote to her husband, 'for I was never more tired and bored than I am with all these ceremonies.' But she remembered the frescoes on which Gentile and Giovanni Bellini were working and showed her aristocratic mettle by asking if she could have a portrait of the Doge which Gentile was painting.

Her second visit, after an eventful few years that saw the birth of her son Federico (whose godfather was Cesare Borgia) and the invasion and partition of Naples by the French and the Spaniards, was made in 1502, this time in company with Elisabetta Gonzaga, both of them travelling *incognito* to escape the distractions of official engagements. Venice was calm, confident, enjoying *la douceur de la vie* before the storm,

They arrived in March to hear that all Venice knew of their presence. After excusing themselves from seeing the Doge, because they had no suitable clothes to wear, they went to hear mass at Ca' Grande and afterwards, Isabella wrote to her husband, 'landed at the Rialto and walked through the fish market and the Merceria to the columns of S. Marco. There were such crowds of people that it was difficult to make our way, but we enjoyed it so much that we did not mind the walk . . .' The next day, they received some gifts from the Signory – including four large boxes of fish, eight large gilt marzipan cakes and twenty pounds of wax candles . . . 'We went to Mass at the Carita, and so on to S. Marco, where the Pala and Treasury were shown us by Messer Paolo Barbo, the procurator. Then we were taken to the Great Hall of the Council, and to the Armoury of the Doge's Palace, after which we went on foot as far as the Rialto, where we took boat and came home to dinner. Afterwards we went to the Arsenal, which our friend Messer Alvise Marcello showed us with the greatest care and kindness . . .'

About all this, the Duchess of Urbino, Isabella told Francesco, 'owns that it is more marvellous than Rome and wonders at the sight . . .'

Isabella d'Este's husband lived dangerously as a *condottiere*, serving Venice, France and the Papacy simultaneously and in turns and involving his family in startlingly intricate diplomatic manoeuvres as alliances changed and the fortunes of war shifted abruptly. In 1508, he joined Julius II, King Louis and the Emperor Maximilian in the League of Cambrai. During the war that followed, when moving with a small band of troops to join the Imperialists in an attack on Padua, he was surprised and captured by Venetian soldiers, and taken in triumph back to Venice. The plunder taken from those with him when he was

The court of Lodovico Gonzaga

caught, wrote da Porto – beautiful horses, splendid armour, clothing, rich furnishings, camp-beds and tents – seemed more suited for a pleasure-trip than a military expedition. In Piazza San Marco there were calls of 'Hang the traitor!' as the marquis was led to be imprisoned in the strong tower of the Doge's Palace.

The family's shattered dignity – there are various accounts of how, to escape capture, Francesco leapt naked through a window and hid in a field of maize – was restored by Isabella who, while the Venetians were hailing the event as a good augury, consulted her astrologers, took over the affairs of state, and sent envoys to the Emperor, the King of France and the Sultan to ask help in securing Francesco's release. After peace had been made between Pope Julius and Venice, on the reversal of alliances that created the Holy League against France, Francesco was freed in 1510.

The next time Venice is seen through the eyes of the Gonzagas, following the shock of Cambrai, with Italy still in turmoil, the same ceremonies, the same courtesies, the same enduring sights

31

and spectacles come into view. Francesco sent his seventeen-year-old Federico to visit the Doge in his stead in May 1517. Among the companions and courtiers who went with him was Baldessar Castiglione, now under the protection of the rulers of Mantua after the capture of his beloved Urbino by the troops of Leo X.

The visitors were escorted in boats from Malamocco on the Lido (the main port of Venice till Napoleon's time) to the Riva degli Schiavoni, lodged in various palaces, and taken the next day to see St Mark's and the Doge's Palace where they were received by Doge Leonardo Loredano. On Ascension Day, after morning mass Federico accompanied the Doge on the *Bucintoro* for the ceremony of the wedding of the sea. Sightseeing for Federico and his friends during their visit took in the Treasury of St Mark's, the glass-works at Murano, and the Arsenal. They rowed in gondolas, were invited to supper parties, and took a light-hearted interest in the balloting for offices at a meeting of the Grand Council.

Two years later, Federico Gonzaga succeeded his father as Marquis of Mantua and became in turn the captain-general of the forces of the Church. In his mid-twenties, dark-haired and hand-some, he loved clothes, horses and women. He is best remem-bered as the patron of Giulio Romano, but also for the support and friendship he extended to Pietro Aretino in a squally rela-tionship that lasted till his death. In 1523, Federico gave Aretino an apartment in his palace in Mantua. 'Being with him', the marquis remarked, 'is like having the company of a whole crowd.'

Later, Aretino became an embarrassment to his host, because of the irritation of the Medici Pope, Clement VII, over his satirical thrusts at the Curia. Aretino became bored with Mantua (though it provided him with the material for his comedy, *The Stablemaster*) and retreated to Venice. The Doge of the time (1523–1538) was Andrea Gritti, a courageous leader who had steadied Venetian morale during the war of the League of Cam-brai, made a forceful role in the 'reconquest' of the mainland territories and was a strong, calm, clever diplomat. He was a friend of architects and writers.

The actual moves that set up the network of relationships that Aretino soon constructed in Venice are not clear, but the part played by Federico Gonzaga must have been influential. Gritti gave Aretino support and protection in return for the favours of his pen. Soon, through the efforts of the Doge or through Jacopo Sansovino or Sebastiano del Piombo (both seeking refuge in Venice in 1527), Aretino had embarked on the mutually affectionate and materially as well as artistically rewarding relationship with Titian that lasted the rest of his life. When the Emperor Charles V – within sight of the final subjection to Imperial power of all Italy save Venice – visited Mantua in 1532, the picture he most admired in the Palace was Titian's portrait of Federico, who immediately –but without instant success – asked Titian to hasten to Mantua (and, he added, to bring some fish with him). Charles V first sat for Titian at Bologna soon after.

Aretino's published letters to Federico from Venice confirm the spirit of commercialism, opportunism, enterprise and courtly patronage that sustained writers and artists in Venice in the sixteenth century.

Isabella d'Este went again to Venice in 1523, twenty-one years after her holiday there with Elisabetta Gonzaga, and she made almost annual visits after 1530. She saw Andrea Gritti being crowned as Doge. She received from Titian portraits, sent at Pietro Aretino's suggestion, of Pietro himself and of a Venetian patrician, the Imperial envoy, Girolamo Adorno. Her portrait was painted by Titian in Mantua and again, in Venice, in 1530.

Isabella d'Este had refused to accompany Federico on his trip to Venice soon after he succeeded Francesco, chiefly, it seems likely, because he took with him a mistress whom she disliked. But her last journey to Venice was made in his company. They stayed for two months in the autumn of 1538 in the palace belonging to his cousin, Ercole d'Este, Duke of Ferrara, on the Grand Canal. Isabella died the next spring; Federico (who had been created Duke of Mantua by the Emperor in 1530) died the year after.

For important impressionable visitors such as the Gonzagas, when their alliance was sought or their friendly service secured, the Venetians paid heavily and put forward the smiling face of their beautiful city. Venice's display of wealth and prosperity was unfeigned. In the sixteenth century, after the convulsions of Cambrai, until the 1570s, Venice increased trade and production; enjoyed long periods of peace and kept secure against attack;

stabilised and entrenched the political power of its patrician class; provided the soil for a brilliant flowering of literature, architecture and painting; reinforced its independence as other Italian states succumbed to French and then Spanish domination, and in a Europe dominated by autocratic nation states and bloodied by religious persecution, earned a reputation for holding liberty, legitimacy, order, tolerance, privilege and the general welfare in steady balance.

On the maintenance of Venice's sea-routes and on secure passage by land depended the equilibrium of the State, the growth of production and trade, and all that flowed from these in social contentment and cultural achievement. The cosmopolitan genius of the Venetians expressed itself in the Renaissance not only through the works of the artists whom they produced or fostered, but also through their creative response to the new arrangements of power and directions of energy in geography, economics, and politics.

The spice trade recovered, both in volume and value.

New markets in the Veneto and abroad absorbed increased production of a widening range of Venetian exports, including woollens, silks, glassware, leather, soap and printed books. The crafts flourished. Magnificent building projects gave Venice its almost completed pattern and shape. Shipbuilding and ship-repairing continued to provide the sinews of the economy and of the State's defence. The land-empire was won back. The sea possessions of Venice remained intact. The Arsenal, with reason, was on every visitor's itinerary: as evidence of the skill of Venice, as a visible sign of resistance against the Turk, and as the formidable spectacle of Europe's biggest industrial enterprise.

From Venice's resilience and recuperation sprang the embellishment of the city state to furnish it with the perpetually changing light and the kaleidoscopic reflections of sea and sky – new images for the visitors who came in increasing numbers. They arrived in search of work, as exiles, looking for patronage and intellectual and artistic stimulus, out of religious impulse or to trade or buy. As High Renaissance forms faded in Rome and Florence, they developed in Venice in lively, experimental literature, in religious reform, in the paintings of Titian, Tintoretto and Veronese, and in the buildings of Sansovino and Palladio.

At the beginning of the sixteenth century, the vigorous fresh-

A page of Virgil printed by Aldus Manutius

ness of Renaissance discovery, mingled with industry and trade, was evident all around in Venice, not only in the paintings of Carpaccio, Giorgione and Bellini, but also in the highly productive and intellectually explosive business of printing.

Among the objects Isabella d'Este sought greedily and ruthlessly for her collections were the books printed by Aldus Manutius. In 1501, she wrote to Lorenzo da Pavia enquiring after the editions of Virgil, Petrarch and Ovid that were being printed in Venice 'in a small size, with minute and almost italic type . . .' Lorenzo in response visited the house of the printer and wrote to tell Isabella of the plans to print Dante, and after Dante, Ovid. Aldus then began to correspond with her direct and, although early on she objected to the price charged for four volumes on vellum – and sent them back – she bought his books and showed him marks of favour.

The printed book was loved for the quality of its paper and the magnificence of its binding as well as for the content and the print. After Castiglione sent the manuscript of his *Book of the Courtier* for printing at the Aldine Press in 1527, he told his steward: 'I am writing to Venice to say that one thousand and thirty copies are to be printed, and that I intend to pay half the expenses, because, of this thousand, five hundred are to be mine. The remaining thirty copies will all belong to me, and are to be printed on fine paper, as smooth and beautiful as possible – in fact, the best that can be found in Venice.' The presentation copies, Castiglione commanded, after his book's publication, were to include one copy for himself on vellum 'with the pages gilded and well pressed, and covered with leather of some rich colour – purple or blue or yellow or green . . . and adorned with ornaments of knots and foliage, or panels and compartments of some other description.'

The boundaries of the businesses of authorship, printing, publishing, bookselling were uncertain, shifting, expanding. Aretino, in a letter to his own printer, Francesco Marcolini, wrote in 1537: 'A writer who goes to the shop in the evening to collect the money from the day's sales smacks of the pimp who empties his woman's purse before he goes to bed.' But his enormous success as a best-selling author played its part in attracting to Venice a new breed of writer anxious to emulate his rich style of living, to share his comparative freedom from censorship, and to hurl their criticism, in the vernacular, at the abuses of ecclesiastical and princely power in contemporary Italy.

During the sixteenth century, Venice kept the lead in the publishing business, whose bookshops and printing houses were grouped mostly in the centre of the city, within easy walking distance of Aretino's house on the water's edge near the Rialto. At mid-century, the printing press in Venice employed about five hundred workers or more, about a quarter of the numbers toiling in the Arsenal. Taking advantage of the city's efficient financing and distribution systems, and the availability of manuscripts, were about fifty publishing enterprises in existence at mid-century, ranging from the large, established firms such as the Aldine Press, the Marcolini and Giunti (specialising in the classics, in religious publications and in secular works respectively) to makeshift little businesses which mushroomed by the score and disappeared. The five hundred or so publishers at work in Venice at one time or another during the century manufactured perhaps as many as twenty million books for sale throughout Italy and abroad.

The prince of printers was Aldus Manutius – Aldo Manuzio in the Italian – always busy, always curious, with a nose for opportunities, a taste for scholarly friendships, and the essential flair of an entrepreneur in assembling the right work force (mostly Greeks from Crete) and spotting technical and artistic talent. He was driven by the vital stimulus of a devouring passion, to spread the knowledge of Greek and promote the reading of reliable editions of the ancient classics. Aldus came originally from Bassiano in the Papal States, and his pursuit of scholarship sprang from his friendship with the great humanist, Pico della Mirandola, who introduced him to the noble family of Carpi which financed his business. The firm lasted till the 1590s when the family petered out after surviving the interruptions of wartime dislocation in the early years of the century and the growth of luxuriant competition.

Aldus set up shop about 1490, when printing from movable type had been well-established in Venice (chiefly by Germans) for nearly twenty years. For scholars between 1495 and 1515 (the year of his death) he produced books in Greek initiated magnificently with five volumes of Aristotle and marching through Aristophanes, Thucydides, Herodotus, Xenophon, Euripides, Desmosthenes, Plutarch, Plato and Pindar. After 1500, for a wider audience, he printed, in beautiful italic type, octavo editions of the series in Latin and Italian that whetted the appetite of Isabella d'Este and continue to excite the emotions of bibliophiles to this day: Virgil first, then Dante, Petrarch, Ovid and Tibullus (the four authors whom Machiavelli was to read in 1513, in exile, when forming the idea of *The Prince*), followed by a muster of the

Aldus Manutius' dolphin and anchor

great Romans, Catullus, Propertius, Horace, Lucan, Juvenal . . .
His new style of book was cheap compared to the price of earlier
productions, scrupulously edited for textual accuracy and simplicity, convenient to hold and carry, and run off on paper or
parchment in big editions for quick sale.

The renowned imprint of the dolphin and anchor, the admirable spectacle of a printing works and household – and a fashionable academy – devoted, under the loving and pious guidance of
Aldus, to the pursuit of classical learning, proved a magnet to
bookmen, collectors, traders and scholars. Eagerly drawn there
was Desiderius Erasmus, in the year 1507.

Erasmus, at the age of thirty-eight, was already famous, an
increasingly controversial, frail and highly sensitive scholar. He
was still recovering from a mistaken vocation to the monastic life
through the therapy of friendship, travel and scholarship that fed
his keen intellectual and determined literary ambition. His
catholic mind and pen ranged critically over politics, religion and
education, and turned instinctively to satire. Like Aretino – the
coarse traces in their writing style often similar, their mode of life
and character miles apart – he held forceful views on the public
issues and expressed them through thousands of letters as well as
his books.

Aretino, in a notable phrase, said that Erasmus had 'enlarged
the confines of human genius', and Erasmus was to exert considerable influence on the religious thinking and literary style of
Aretino's followers, thanks not least to the printer, Aldus Manutius.

When he met Aldus, he had already published the first edition
of his *Adages*, a collection of classical sayings with explanations
and commentaries; his most important religious work, the
Enchiridion; and, in collaboration with Thomas More, several
translations of Lucian. The *Enchiridion* had been strongly
influenced by the neo-Platonic philosophy of Aldus's patron,
Pico della Mirandola.

Erasmus travelled in Italy during 1506–1509, for a year as
tutor to the two sons of Henry VII's physician, an Italian from
Genoa. In this company he was forced on one occasion to flee
from Bologna to Florence, as the Papal armies swept towards it
in attack under the leadership of Pope Julius II and Francesco
Gonzaga, Marquis of Mantua.

It was from Bologna, in October 1507, that he wrote to Aldus Manutius. He had often wished, he said, that the light Manutius had cast on Greek and Latin literature 'not by your printing alone and your splended types, but by your brilliance and your uncommon learning' could be matched by the profit the printer earned. He enquired whether Manutius would be publishing Plato and the New Testament. Meanwhile, he was sending to Aldus two tragedies he had translated from Euripedes, which had been badly printed and which, he thought, would immortalise his labours 'if they could come out printed in your types, particularly the smaller types, the most beautiful of all.' If Aldus insisted on his taking a hundred or two volumes himself, added Erasmus, 'though the God of gain does not usually favour me' he would do so provided a horse were fixed as the price.

As a result of their correspondence, Erasmus and Aldus agreed that the former should visit Venice, not only to supervise the printing of the translations, but also to supervise the printing of an enlarged edition of the *Adages*.

According to Erasmus's early biographer, Beatus Rhenanus, his first hours in Venice were dismally embarrassing. He arrived at the Aldine offices and was kept waiting for a long time 'either because Aldus was busy supervising the work of the printers hurriedly putting together the metal type, or because he thought that it was one of those regular visitors who kept coming more out of curiosity than to offer help and were always troublesome . . . When he knew it was Erasmus, he begged his pardon and embraced him tenderly, and kept him with him in the house of Andrea Asolano, its [the Press's] famous owner and his own father-in-law.'

Erasmus and Aldus worked together on preparing the *Adages* for the press, the former writing proof corrections up to the last minute, the latter also reading the proofs because, he said, he was studying at the same time.

In Venice, at the New Academy founded by Manutius, Erasmus came to know a group of scholars who helped him add to his collection of classical sayings as they went to press; he practised his Greek; he explored the riches of his host's library; and he saw the manuscript of the newly discovered *Pervigilium Veneris*.

Many years later, in his *Colloquia familiaria*, a series of discussions on politics and religion in dialogue form, Erasmus

39

scandalised some of his contemporaries by acid recollections of his time in Venice. At the house near the Rialto of Andrea Asolanus he recalled, you would find a group of learned men sharing a meal of 'seven tiny lettuce leaves swimming in vinegar . . .'

The attack came in a chapter called *Opulentia sordida*, an account of a miserly household, in which Andrea Asolanus is not at all disguised under the name of Antronius, and Aldus is Orthrogonus.

In Antronius's house, while the north wind was blowing, damp roots were used for firewood. In the summer, the house was teeming with fleas and bed-bugs. To drink, you were given bad wine mixed with water and dregs. The bread was made from mouldy wheat, and you could hardly break it with your teeth when it appeared at supper. Breakfast was never mentioned in that house. When Antronius wanted to pose as a Lucullus, then on the table would appear a *minestra* of water and buffalo cheese, and a scrap of tired tripe.

'Every nation has its own custom. The Italians spend little on drink; they prefer money to pleasure and are sober by nature as well as habit.'

After mentioning 'a thin little chicken', Erasmus, with Lucianic suggestiveness, puts into the mouth of James (who is conducting this particular dialogue with Gilbert) the remark: 'Yet I hear of a kind of bird there that's very plentiful, choice, and cheap.'

'True,' Gilbert replies, 'but they love money more . . .'

And finally: 'The scarcity of the food did not bother me so much . . . as the badness of it.'*

Erasmus always blamed his kidney stone on the poor wine he was given to drink at the house of Aldus Manutius's father-in-law. But he was also paying off old scores arising from a rumbustious literary quarrel with an Italian humanist and physician, Julius Caesar Scaliger, who had mauled him over his inferior Latin style and accused him of being a drunkard in his Venetian days. Erasmus suspected in his onslaught the hand of a former friend he had known in Venice and resorted to general ridicule of his Venetian hosts. Allowing for poetic spite, his sketches of domestic life in Venice realistically balance the blaze of public splendour.

* Cf. *The Colloquies of Erasmus* translated by Craig R. Thompson (University of Chicago Press 1965).

Erasmus also recalled that the nobles of Venice shaved their heads. In contrast with Germany, where foreigners are stared at, in Venice (as in Rome and Paris) 'nothing causes surprise'. The Venetians arrange magnificent funerals. For a minumum of expense, any cobbler would have a splendid burial, with a fine bier provided by his guild; 'and sometimes six hundred monks, dressed in tunics and cloaks, accompany a single corpse.'

In her study 'The "Adages" of Erasmus' Margaret Mann Phillips reconstructs evocatively the magical moment of the discovery of the *Pervigilium Veneris* in its Renaissance context.

'One can imagine the two of them, Aldus and Erasmus, in a room in Venice, poring over the manuscript in the mellow Venetian light. They were reading for the first time the *Pervigilium Veneris*, and its nostalgic recall of the spring of the heart evoked by the song of the nightingale: *Illa cantat, nos tacemus; quando ver venit meum?* This seems fitting, for it was with a nostalgia of their own that they looked back to the flowering of the past, and forward to another springtime of learning and poetry.'

Discovery of Venice won its savour for Erasmus from the quality of Aldus's library, from being able to converse there with a select and learned company of scholars in the Greek he loved, from seeing the young patricians of the city (as he later recalled in one of the adages noting the fashion of wearing trousers for the first time and showing them off): 'who whenever they travel abroad take delight in wearing the French shirt without a coat over it, a thing they do not do at home.' When he was older, the rapture faded, not only because of the bitter attacks from Italy on his alleged Lutheranism, but also because there were now too many books, too shoddily edited. 'They fill the world with books, not just trifling things (such as I perhaps write) but stupid, ignorant, slanderous, raving, irreligious and seditious books.'

The books from the Aldine Press were scholarly, mostly classical. Other publishers by the hundred were responsible for the flood of books, by contemporary authors, of the sort that came to scandalise Erasmus. Among them, though eminently respectable, was Francesco Marcolini, from Forlì who specialised in works in the vernacular by authors such as Anton Francesco Doni, letter-writer, editor and printer himself, and who published

The Miracle of the Cross

the books of the influential architect, Sebastiano Serlio. One of
Marcolini's authors was that tempest of a man, Pietro Aretino.

Venice had been a revelation for Aretino when he settled there,
in his mid-thirties, in 1527, the year of the sack of Rome, after an
adventurous career whose current alternated between indulgent
patronage and fame and dangerous disrepute and disgrace, at the
Curia, in camp with the heroic *condottiere* Giovanni delle Bande
Nere, and at the Court of Mantua. He was in Venice for over a
quarter of a century, till his death in 1556, living for most of the
time in a rented house on the Grand Canal. In Venice he found
friends in both high and low life, to suit his varied tastes; an
efficient printing press able to cope with his voluminous output
of market-oriented writing; and an exceptional freedom, for the
Europe of the time, of artistic and literary expression. He lived in
a physical environment of fantastic beauty and great wealth. The

volumes of Aretino's letters which were published in Venice between 1537–1557 contain the kind of descriptions, the single descriptive phrases, which make one exclaim: that was how it must have been. The subject matter is rich and varied: the important political events of the time, such as the imprisonment of the French king; the day-to-day incidents of his own life, a love-affair gone wrong or a gift of salad or wine; advice to a young man about getting married or becoming a soldier; tender thoughts on golden-hearted prostitutes or his own baby daughter. With occasional flights of bombast and rhetoric, the letters are the observant reports of a brilliant journalist: witty, detailed, colourful. Not only the glittering surface life of Venice is there, for they mark also the boundaries of the tolerance extended to the writers of the time and through their subject-matter and flattery indicate the preoccupations of contemporary Venetians and the image that Venice entertained of itself.

A letter of Aretino's addressed to the Doge Andrea Gritti, written in 1530, exalts Venice as a haven of freedom, as a champion of Italian patriotism, and as a model of good government. 'Here treachery has no place, here reigns neither the cruelty of harlots nor the insolence of the effeminate, here there is no theft, or violence, or murder . . . O universal homeland! Custodian of the liberties of man! Refuge of exiles!'

In the same letter, Venice is praised as being 'more resplendent than any city ever was'. Aretino, who grew up with painters and poets, and wanted to be an artist when he was young, uses a painter's eye and perception to describe the daily life of Venice, the activities of artists and writers, bishops and patricians, ambassadors and scholars, priests and peasants, boatmen and shopkeepers, particular colours, smells, tastes, against the background of the light and shade of water and sky and the solidities and reflections of its monuments and buildings. The revelation of Venice as a unique theatre of nature and stage of human life, mirrored by so many writers and painters since, is contained most expressively in two letters written respectively to his landlord Domenico Bollani (the Venetian diplomat and patrician who later became Bishop of Brescia) and his intimate friend Titian.

'Time flows when you rest your elbows on the ledges of Venetian windows,' Henry James was to say a few hundred years after Aretino, who contemplated the scene from his window and wrote in 1537:

'Never do I lean out of the windows but I see at market time a thousand persons and as many gondolas. In my field of vision to the right stand the Fish Market and the Meat Market; in the space to the left, the Bridge and the Fondaco dei Tedeschi; where both views meet I see the Rialto, packed with merchants. I have grapes in the barges, game and game birds in the shops, vegetables on the pavement . . . It is all fascinating, including the twenty or twenty-five sailboats, choked with melons, which are lashed together to make a kind of island where people run and assess the quality of the melons by snuffing them and weighing them . . . But let me tell you I split my sides laughing when the hoots, whistles and shouts of the boatman explode behind those who are rowed along by servants who aren't wearing scarlet breeches. And who wouldn't have pissed himself on seeing capsize in the bittermost cold a boat packed with Germans just escaped from the tavern . . .'

And in 1544:

'As I am describing it, see first the buildings which appeared to be artificial though made of real stone. And then look at the air itself, which I perceived to be pure, and consider my wonder at the clouds made up of condensed moisture; in the principal vistas they were partly near the roofs of the buildings, and partly on the horizon, while to the right all was in a confused shading of greyish-black. I was awestruck by the varieties of colours they displayed: the nearest glowed with the flames of the sun's fire; the furthest were blushing with the brightness of partially burnt vermillion. Oh, how beautiful were the strokes with which Nature's brushes pushed the air back at this point, separating it from the palaces in the way that Titian does when painting his landscapes! In some places, the colours were green-blue, and in others they appeared blue-green, finely mixed by the whims of Nature, who is the teacher of teachers. With light and shades, they gave deep perspective and high relief to what she wished to bring forward and set back, and so I, who knows how your brush breathes with her spirit, cried out three or four times: "Oh, Titian, where are you?"
   '"Oh, Tiziano, dove sete mo?"'

After the death of Aldus Manutius his two brothers-in-law and old Andrea ran the business in rather a mediocre fashion till it was handed over to Aldo's son Paolo in 1533. He produced mostly editions of the classics, notably Cicero, and then migrated to Rome leaving in charge his own son in turn who, said Erasmus's enemy Scaliger (who seems to have had a bad word to say about everyone) produced commonplace work and aped his father.

The second Aldo Manuzio died in 1597. While the glories of the Aldine Press were fading away, the Venice to which their original work added such a blaze of intellectual and artistic distinction was physically transformed. Sansovino's three beautiful palaces, his Library, the Fabbriche Nuove and the Mint; the new Rialto bridge, humped in stone and cluttered with shops; Palladio's airy San Giorgio Maggiore and the Redentore were in process of building or completed by the end of the century. The images of Venice grew richer and more complex, as did the reception of the idea of Venice in the imaginations of those who visited the city or heard of its fame. In the north, Venice inspired curiosity and speculation because of its reputation for good, enduring government and for the balance it preserved between its age-old Catholicism and its semi-mystical independence as a state. In hindsight, dwarfed by the power of the Empire and the emergent nation states of Europe (though Queen Elizabeth railed in her old age against the Venetians because the Signory had sent her no ambassador during her reign), Venice was still seen, despite the double-dealing of centuries, as a bulwark against the Turk.

Regatta for women

Joachim du Bellay, the most magical of the poets of the French Renaissance, who spent nearly five years in Italy about mid-century, described the sights of Venice:

Leur superbe arcenal, leur vaisseaux, leur abbord,
Leur Saint-Marc, leur Palais, leur Realte, leur port,
Leurs changes, leurs profits, leur banque & leurs trafiques . . .
Mais ce que l'on en doit le meilleur estimer,
C'est quand ces vieux coquz vont espouser la mer,
Dont ils sont les maris & le Turc l'adultere.

[*Their superb arsenal, their ships, their landing,*
Their Saint Mark, their Palace, their Rialto, their port,
Their exchanges, their profits, their bank, and their trade . . .
But what one should esteem above all,
Is when those old cuckolds set out to wed the sea,
Of which they are the husbands, and the Turk the adulterer.]

The truth, however, was nearer what the Grand Vizier told a Venetian envoy in 1499, after Venice's defeat by the Turks at sea and on land: 'Tell your Doge that up to the present he has wedded the sea; it will be our turn in future, for we own more of the sea than he does . . .'

On 7 October 1571, Don John of Austria, the illegitimate, much favoured son of the Emperor Charles V, half-brother to King Philip of Spain, led the Christian fleets of Spain, Genoa, Venice and the Papacy through a four-hour battle to a resounding and gory victory over the Turks in the Gulf of Corinth. Good fortune, Providence and prayer no doubt, skilful deployment of the ships, and broadside fire brought triumph at Lepanto and the sea was violated with blood and wreckage. Estimates differ, but over twenty-five thousand Turks were killed or drowned; perhaps over ten thousand Christians died; and twenty thousand Christian galley slaves were freed from the holds. Among the wounded was Miguel Cervantes, who returned to Spain to write *Don Quixote* and to recall the battle in the story of 'The Captive'.

The Holy League against the Ottoman Empire had been organised in Venice, Rome and Madrid in response to the Turkish assault on Cyprus. Ottoman power in the Mediterranean would still advance, but its surge forward was decisively checked and its morale enfeebled. In an ignoble peace treaty in 1573, nonetheless, as the alliance crumbled, after centuries of Venetian domination Cyprus was ceded to the Turks and the Venetians paid a hefty indemnity.

After Lepanto, Europe rejoiced. The news came first to Venice, brought swiftly by a galley called *The Angel* spied on 18 October sailing towards the Lido, firing cannon, trailing Turkish colours, with turbans piled on the deck. The exuberant celebrations included the commissioning of paintings by Tintoretto and Veronese. Veronese's huge allegorical picture was completed in 1578 for the newly reconstructed *Sala di Collegio* where the Doges received ambassadors. It showed Sebastiano Venier, the admiral of the Venetian fleet at Lepanto, kneeling before Christ in thanks for the victory. The painting is a triumphantly organised attestation of the enduring impulses in Venice towards a fusion of patriotic fervour, Christian orthodoxy, and imperial assertion.

When Sir Philip Sidney arrived in Venice in 1573 the sense of achievement from Lepanto glowed strongly. The last decades of the century brought renewal as well as completion. In 1574 after fire had spread through the centre of the city and gutted parts of the Doge's Palace, restoration work started on the halls of the Senate and the Collegio and the Doge's private apartments which were soon to receive rich decorations and paintings by Tintoretto and Veronese and Palma. Plague struck in 1575 and killed about fifty thousand of the hundred and ninety thousand inhabitants of the lagoon, including Titian who in 1576 was

Sir Philip Sidney

buried in the great Franciscan church of the Frari: the law forbidding the burial of plague victims in city churches was set aside for him. When the contagion abated, in thanksgiving the Venetians commissioned from Palladio the design of the serenely classical church of the Redentore, on the Giudecca, across a sheet of water and in mood and setting apart from the heart of the city, a monument to great Venetian families and patrons, to Venetian nostalgia for Rome and to religious faith.

Sir Philip Sidney's view of Venice was shadowed and stressed by romantic protestantism. Roger Ascham's *The Schoolmaster*, published in 1570, told him and other young Englishmen what to expect of Italy. In Italy, the diatribe said, good English protestants risked being transformed into licentious papists. 'I was once in Italy myself, but I thank God my abode there was but nine days; and yet I saw in that little time, in one city, more liberty to sin than ever I heard tell of in our noble city of London in nine year . . .'

Venice was the city where it was free to sin 'not only without all punishment, but also without any man's marking, as it is as free in the city of London to choose without any blame whether a man lust to wear shoe or pantocle . . . I learned when I was at Venice that there it is counted good policy when there be four or five brethren of one family, one only to marry, and all the rest to waulter with as little shame in open lechery as swine do here in the common mire.'

For Sidney, and the growing stream of visitors from England during the following years, Venice was attractive as a centre of intellectual stimulus. It held Padua under its rule and there the university flourished, attracting scholars from all over Europe, amassing a great artistic as well as legal and classical tradition. Venice was also fascinating as a political model to be studied, if not admired, and a Catholic city, sometimes shaking free of the embraces of the Vatican, on neutral ground, but darkly part of the Italian menace.

The massacre of St Bartholomew which took place when Sidney himself was in Paris added a thrill of physical threat to the sense of spiritual temptation.

Sidney was nineteen when he left his fond friend and correspondent the French protestant lawyer and political agent, Hubert Languet, in Germany and travelled to Venice. He had left England for the continent in order to learn foreign languages. He was serious, full of charm and good looks. Languet's life and Sidney's intertwined, in affection and correspondence, through common friends and purposes. Languet had been a professor of law at Padua. He became a protestant under the influence of Melanchthan; he too was in Paris at the time of the St Bartholomew's Day massacre; his friendship with Sidney ripened when they both stayed at Frankfurt with the printer Wechel. And Wechel was to give hospitality some years later to Giordano Bruno, before Bruno's journey to Venice, imprisonment and eventual burning in Rome.

Sidney promised Languet that he would write once a week from Italy (the promise was not quite fulfilled) and his letters from Venice and Padua, over a period of eight months, are sharp and fresh but provoke rather than satisfy the imagination.

Sidney travelled in winter on horseback with his companions across the Alps. The season may explain why he apparently found little of interest to write to Languet about. Just before Christmas 1573 his Burgundian friend wrote to him: 'I judge from your letter that the splendour of Venice does not equal your expectations; nevertheless Italy has nothing fit to be compared to it, so that if this does not please you, the rest will disgust you . . .'

In Padua, in January 1574, Sidney pursued his languages, turning Cicero into French and then English and 'by a sort of perpetual motion' into Latin again, and having Paolo Manuzio help him with Italian. In February, he wrote to Languet about his intention of having a portrait done. 'As soon as ever I return to Venice, I will have it done either by Paul Veronese, or by Tintoretto, who hold by far the highest place in the art . . .'

From Venice, on 26 February, Sidney wrote: 'This day one Paul of Verona has begun my portrait, for which I must stay here two or three days longer.'

The portrait was sent to Languet who wrote immediately that it looked too young for Sidney, rather like his brother, but a year later that he had framed it, placed it in a conspicuous place and found it 'so beautiful, and so strongly to resemble you, that I possess nothing which I value more . . . The painter has represented you a little sad and thoughtful.'

The portrait, alas, is lost. Veronese, the pupil of Titian and rival of Tintoretto, was in his early forties when Sidney met him, and very popular as a portrait painter. He was probably the better

49

choice for Sidney, the epitome of the courtier, in which character as in the art of Veronese were mingled gravity, sweetness, nobility, nonchalance.

Sidney's love and knowledge of painting, stimulated presumably through his contact with Veronese, are evident in his later writing; so too the intimacy he gained with Italian poetry and philosophy. From Venice, though, he wrote austerely about his experiences, perhaps too conscious of Languet's jealous eye for his heart and mind. In April, he wrote, rather callowly, that it might be a good thing if the Turks came into Italy. 'First of all that rotten member will be removed, which has now so long infected the whole Christian body . . . I am convinced that this baneful Italy would so contaminate the very Turks, would so ensare them with all its vile allurements, that they would soon fall down of themselves . . .'

The 'vile allurements' both men saw as chiefly Popery, then the false Italian charm. In July 1577 Languet remarked in a letter to his young friend: 'What wonder if the court of Rome can beguile a young prince with its sorceries, when it has so stifled the Venetians, who think themselves the wisest of men, that they have suffered the Inquisition to be established in their city . . .'

In a letter to his brother, Robert, Sidney a few years following his Italian visit noted the 'good laws and customs' of the Venetians – in contrast to the rest of Italy – but suggested that they could not be relevant to England 'because they are quite of a contrary government.'

At Venice, he discussed politics. He read the works of Cardinal Contarini and Donato Gianotti, on government and history. He learned horsemanship. He became an enthusiast for the creation of *imprese* – devices and mottoes – for gentlemen to wear. Above all, instructed by the *Poetice* of Julius Caesar Scaliger, his eye and intellect trained by contemplation of paintings in Venice, his literary techniques extended by his immersion in Italian poetry, Sidney brought back from Venice the experiences and disposition that would create the sonnets, *The Defence of Poesy* and the *Arcadia* before he died, after battle, from a wound in the thigh, at the age of thirty-two.

Basilius, king of *Arcadia*, is described by Sidney in one scene as listening to the music of Zelmane, then 'falling down upon both his knees and holding up his hands, as the old governess of Danae is painted when she suddenly saw the golden shower . . .'. As she is painted indeed by Titian and other Renaissance painters. Sidney's poetry is full of such images inspired by pictures and performing in words the functions of paintings. His own life suggests a series of representations in oils, of idealised and courtly Renaissance scenes, the fruit of Castiglione's inspired glosses on life at Urbino and England's cult of the Virgin Queen. Sidney, a young and beautiful aristocrat, sitting for Veronese; courteously greeting when on diplomatic business for the queen in 1577, the then harassed, heroic Don John of Austria, governor-general of the Netherlands; gallantly handing a wounded soldier his flask to drink from when mortally wounded himself.

The marvel is the creative seeding achieved by Italy of the genius of Sidney (despite crude religious fear and prejudice) and therefore through emulation and rivalry the influence of the Italians on the whole course of England's literary Renaissance.

My images of Renaissance Venice have moved away from the

city, with the crack ringing-out of the musket shot that ended Sir Philip Sidney's life and the crackling of the fire that killed Giordano Bruno in Rome. For Venice itself, scenes of violence seem to pack the first and last years of the century. There appears to be no peace in Venice, but constant movements and action stirred by war, plague and social and religious restlessness, as well as by the working out of the consequences of new inventions and discoveries – in art and literature, in political theory, in printing and painting, in the techniques of navigation and manufacture.

The frenzy of activity in sixteenth-century Venice was counterpointed by contemplation and quietness. This balance is a key to the adjustment of Venice during the Renaissance, as defeat and change provoked action and reform. In music, the strife was expressed and resolved.

Vasari tells us of Veronese's painting of 'Music' which won the ambitious young artist the prize of a golden chain from the Signory, under the judgement of Titian and Sansovino, to adorn the fabulous library left to the State by Cardinal Bessarion. It shows three handsome young women, one playing the viola, another the lute, and the third singing from a book. Nearby, a Cupid plays the harpsichord, to show that music engenders love; and Pan plays his pipes. In their pictures, Veronese and other painters from Bellini to Titian, showed their appreciation of music and their intimate knowledge of musical instruments.

Throughout the century, at San Marco, a permanent group of singers, instrumentalists and the organist of the *cappella* wrested the lead for Venice in performances and compositions and, refining their inheritance from the Netherlands and to some extent from the East, in turn influenced the development of religious and secular music elsewhere in Europe. And when Veronese was working in Venice, from the 1550s, the madrigal was evolving from its Flemish and Venetian origins into brilliant representational art in words and chords, into serious, complex musical forms.

In *Culture and Society in Venice*, Oliver Logan writes: 'The personal connections of the great musicians of St Mark's are indicative of the role played by music in Venetian society. On the one hand, music, as exemplified by Zarlino, was an erudite study closely allied to mathematics, with a secure place in the world of the learned academics. On the other hand, musical performance was bound up not only with the whole framework of imposing civil and religious celebrations but also with the gay and even bohemian aspects of Venetian life, with the world of the great festive companies and of the theatre.'

Visitors to Venice heard music poured out to celebrate the victory of Lepanto and the triumphal celebration given in the dead of night to the exotic Henry III, King of France and Poland, on his State visit in 1574.

To my mind, the haunting picture of the *Tempest* by Giorgione (in the *Accademia*) holding a breathless moment of stillness before storm, points to the tensions between classicism and romanticism, reality and myth, contemplation and activity that were characteristic of sixteenth-century Venice. It leads one to open the pages of Walter Pater's little book on the Renaissance, and to the essay on the school of Giorgione, where, in describing the picture, putting forward his own *fin de siècle* aesthetic theory, he reminds us too of the creative silence of Venice, broken both by music – including the sweet or coarse verses in Venetian dialogue sung by gondoliers, composed by nobles – and also by the ever-continuing actions of everyday life.

'It is to the law or condition of music, as I said, that all art like this is really aspiring; and, in the school of Giorgione, the perfect moments of music itself, the making or hearing of music, song or its accompaniment, are themselves prominent as subjects. On that background of the silence of Venice, so impressive to the modern visitor, the world of Italian music was then forming. In choice of subject, as in all besides, the *Concert of the Pitti Palace* is typical of everything that Giorgione, himself an admirable musician, touched with his influence. In sketch or finished picture, in various collections, we may follow it through many intricate variations – men fainting at music; music at the pool-side while people fish, or mingled with the sound of the pitcher in the well, or heard across running water, or among the flocks; the tuning of instruments; people with intent faces, as if listening, like those described by Plato in an ingenious passage of the *Republic*, to detect the smallest interval of musical sound, the smallest undulation in the air, or feeling for music in thought on a stringless instrument, ear and finger refining themselves infinitely in the appetite for sweet sound; a momentary touch of an instrument in the twilight, as one passes through some unfamiliar room, in a chance company.'

3 Song and Survival: the Age of the Baroque

Historians tend to pass judgement on centuries in the censorious manner of schoolmasters writing reports. 'Could try harder.' 'A sad deterioration in performance.' Italy, perhaps for having shown such promise in the Renaissance, is especially subjected to the discipline of this approach. So is Venice.

The chapter on the seventeenth century in Giuliano Procacci's compactly brilliant *History of the Italian People* (Penguin Books) is headed with no-nonsense decisiveness: 'A Century of Stagnation'. Successes won by Venice against the Slavonic pirates of the Adriatic were among 'the last true demonstrations of independent initiative' by the Italian states. For Venice, as for other parts of Italy, 'the characteristic rhythm of economic enterprises is a sharp fall followed by a stagnation that goes on for the rest of the century.' Procacci quotes relevant production figures.

A lover of Venice – the author of the most informative and oddly charming of all the guide-books – Giulio Lorenzetti (*Venice and its Lagoon*: Edizioni LINT Trieste) lists moments of glory but nonetheless discerns in the history of the city in the seventeenth century a 'fatal slipping into decadence, that led slowly to her end . . .'

This is not how it struck seventeenth-century Venetians, or those who then travelled in Italy.

My collection of English translations from the Italian 'classics' includes a boldly printed copy of William Aglionby's 'Painting Illustrated in Three Dialogues' together with a rendering of some of Vasari's *Lives* of the painters. (It was published late in the century, in 1685, and dedicated to the notorious William Cavendish, Duke of Devonshire, punter, brawler and politician.) Phrases from the 'Dialogues' (which urge the English who have to spend a lot of time indoors on account of the climate to spend more of it looking at pictures and less over their claret) show how Italy's reputation was well sustained abroad: at least in the arts.

'Painting,' says Aglionby (in the *persona* of 'Traveller' talking to 'Friend') 'is still the greatest charm of the "most polite part" of Mankind . . .'

Merchants at the Rialto

And who are they?

'I mean chiefly the Italians, to whom none can deny the Priviledge of having been the Civilisers of Europe, since Painting, Sculpture, Architecture, Music, Gardening, polite conversation, and prudent behaviour are, as I may call it, all the Growth of their Countrey . . .'

During the seventeenth and early eighteenth centuries, John Hale writes in *England and the Italian Renaissance*, 'interest in Italian history remained uncritical, spasmodic and sensational'. But, as the idea of a Grand Tour began to shape as a necessary part of the education of an English gentleman, visitors to Venice took back the stray thought, or the stimulus, the memory, the contact, the revelation, the image that affected and sometimes transformed their art, their thinking, their lives. They went as scholars, tutors, merchants, diplomats, not yet so often simply as tourists. Among them were Thomas Hobbes, James Howell, Richard Lessels, William Harvey, John Milton, John Evelyn and Gilbert Burnet.

The visitor to seventeenth-century Venice found a city of

Gondolas crashing

dense and resplendent beauty, whose creative sap was still rising, and whose moral qualities were being tested and strengthened. The seventeenth century saw the architectural 'completion' of Venice; its musical triumph in the flowering of opera; a steadying of nerve and consolidation of institutions that impressed men of the world and men of the time whatever future historians would think.

Among the strands woven into the history of Venice in the seventeenth century are Christian belief and civic pride; austerity; love of sensuous beauty; artistic originality; political conservatism. 'The records of Venice in this century,' John Arthos comments in his book on *Milton and the Italian Cities*, 'give a picture of a kind of integrity and harmony. Everything seems to be part of a single way of meeting life . . . It was a city in which the piety of Sarpi, a persistent quietism, and in the most significant sense an official piety – the piety of office – was felt everywhere.'

Opinionated and garrulous, a mini-Falstaff come to judgement, Thomas Coryat took the air in Venice, and wrote about it vividly in English for his countrymen (later, he promised, his work would be put into Latin for others) at the beginning of the age of baroque, between old and new miracles of art.

Coryat travelled on the Continent in 1608 when James I was King of England and Leonardo Donato was Doge of Venice. He was the son of a clergyman (the prebendary of York Cathedral), came from Odcombe, in Somerset, had been educated at Oxford and, in the houschold of the young Prince of Wales, Henry Frederick, seems to have acted the part of entertainer and buffoon. In 1611 he published the account of his walking tour in Europe, prefaced by a bizarre collection of verses in mock praise of the author, apparently ordered by the warmly admired and gifted Prince of Wales to help sell the book. The verses, in several styles and languages, included ingeniously facetious and suggestive lines by Ben Jonson, John Donne, William Fenton, Thomas Campion, John Chapman and Michael Drayton. The names are a tantalising pointer to what might have been, had Prince Henry lived beyond eighteen.

Coryat died at Surat, in the East, when on another of his remarkable expeditions, in 1617, from drinking sack on a weak stomach. ('Sack, sack . . . I pray give me some sack,' he cried out, when he heard it had been brought in by some English visitors.) He had hung the shoes he wore when he left Venice in the parish church at Odcombe, and had given his book the title: *Coryat's Crudities. Hastily gobled up in five moneths travells in France, Savoy, Italy, Rhetia commonly called the Grisons country, Helvetia alias Switzerland, some parts of Germany and the Netherlands; Newly digested in the hungry aire of Odcombe in the County of Somerset, and now dispersed to the nourishment of the travelling Members of this Kingdome.*

Coryat signs his epistle to the reader: 'The Odcombian Legge-stretcher.' Ben Jonson says in a note on his character: 'He is an Engine, wholly consisting of extremes, a Head, Fingers, and Toes. For what his industrious Toes have trod, his ready Fingers have written, his subtle head dictating. He was set a going for Venice the fourteenth of May, anno 1608, and returned home (of himselfe) the third of October following, being wound up for five moneths or thereabouts; his paises two for one . . .'

None of this raillery and bathos prepare the reader of *Coryat's Crudities* for the modest intelligence of his observations, the judiciousness of his choice of detail, or the enthusiasm and pleasing ornateness of his prose when, in a crowning chapter of the book, quoting some verses by Julius Caesar Scaliger, he gives his 'Observations of the most glorious, peerelesse, and mayden Citie of Venice'.

He walked there from Padua – a 'sweete emporium and mart town of learning', with at least one thousand and five hundred students – and that, he recorded, brought his journey from Odcombe, Somerset, to a total of nine hundred and fifty two miles.

He calls her the 'fairest Lady, yea the richest Paragon and Queene of Christendome', in regard of her incomparable situation, surpassing wealth, and most magnificent buildings.

Coryat was anxious to tell his readers the kind of explicit detail omitted from former books. The palaces along the Grand Canal, 'made in the form of a Roman S', for example, were 'of a great height three or foure stories high, most being built with bricke, and some few with faire free stone. Besides, they are adorned with a great multitude of stately pillers made partly of white stone, and partly of Istrian marble. Their roofes doe much differ from those of our English buildings. For they are all flat and built in that manner as men may walke upon them, as I have often observed.'

About the middle of the front of these palaces, he observed, are little terraces with marble or stone balconies 'that people may from that place as from a most delectable prospect contemplate and view the parts of the City round about them in the coole evening.'

The finest bridge with only one arch that Coryat ever heard of was the Rialto, costing about fourscore thousand crowns or four and twenty thousand pounds sterling. The thirteen ferries of Traghetti, he reported severely, were attended by boatmen who proved to be the 'most vicious and licentious varlets about all the City'.

'For if a stranger entereth into one of their Gondolas, and doth not presently tell them whither he will goe, they will incontinently carry him of their owne accord to a religious house forsooth, where his plumes shall be well pulled before he commeth forth againe.'

Perhaps the loquacious and argumentative Englishman asked for trouble. He spent some hours in Venice disputing with a Rabbi in the Ghetto, of which he gives a bigoted but fascinating description, and had to be rescued from an angry crowd of forty or fifty Jews by the secretary of the British ambassador, Sir Henry Wotton, who happened to be passing in his gondola.

Coryat saw the Venetian merchants at the Rialto, at their twice-daily meetings, between eleven and twelve in the morning and five and six in the afternoon. He admired the covered gondolas with their black leather benches and emblems of dolphins' tails, of which he had heard there were ten thousand about the city, six thousand belonging to gentlemen and four thousand plying for hire. He wondered at the Library of Cardinal Bessarion with its 'little world of memorable antiquities made of Alabaster' and at the statues in the Duke's Palace, the glorious view from the Tower of St Mark's. For the cost of a 'gazet', Coryat urged, a single penny, one should see the whole model and form of the city: 'their streetes, their Churches, their

59

Monasteries, their market places, and all their other publike buildings of rare magnificence. Also many faire gardens replenished
with diversity of delicate fruites, as Oranges, Citrons, Lemmons,
Apricocks, muske melons, anguriaes, and what not; together
with their little Islands bordering about the citie wonderfully
frequented and inhabited with people, being in number fifty or
there about. Also the Alpes that lead into Germany . . . and those
that leade into France . . .'

Coryat tells a story of the accident at the clock-tower of St
Mark's Square when the fellow in charge was busy on repairs and
'one of those wilde men that at the quarters of the howers doe use
to strike the bell, strooke the man in the head with his brazen
hammer, giving him such a violent blow, that therewith he fel
down dead presently in the place, and never spake more.' He
could not vouch for this, because he was in the Duke's Palace at
the time. He saw with his own eyes, however, the porphyry stone
by the Palace, for exposing traitors' heads, and the alabaster
gallows for hanging traitorous Doges. He admired the Mint and
its thirty-one money chests, with coins of gold, silver and brass.

After describing the galleries, wells and staircases of the
Doge's Palace, Coryat extolled the Council Hall as 'the fairest
that ever I saw in my life, either in mine owne countrey, or
France, or any city of Italy, or afterward in Germany.' Among
the pictures in the Palace he remarked the battle of Lepanto
'where the Christian fleete got that most glorious victory of the
Turkes . . .'

Before the façade of St Mark's, Coryat stared at the four
bronze horses, which the Venetians had refused to sell to the
King of Spain despite the offer of their weight in gold, but failed
to visit the Treasury, he sadly admits, and so reports only by
hearsay that 'no treasure whatsoever in any one place of Christendome may compare with it . . . Here they say is kept marvellous abundance of rich stones of exceeding worth, as Diamonds,
Carbuncles, Emerauds, Chrysolites, Jacinths, and great
pearles . . .'

On the Arsenal, Coryat quotes the general of the imperial
forces in Italy as saying that it was the eighth wonder of the
world, and if he had to be lord of the four strongest cities in Italy
or of the Arsenal, he would prefer the Arsenal. One thousand five
hundred men worked there; two hundred and fifty galleys were

always kept there, another fifty being always at sea. The fairest was the *Bucintoro*, 'the richest gallie of all the world', used for the ceremony of the betrothal of the sea and surpassed only by the galleys of Cleopatra and of the Emperor Caligula, and 'that most incomparable and peerelesse ship of our Gracious Prince called the Prince Royall, which was launched at Wollige about Michaelmas last . . .'

The centrepiece of Coryat's ecstatic description of Venice was the Piazza of St Mark's; the 'Market Place' of the world, rather than of just the city, where 'you may both see all the manner of fashions of attire, and heare all the languages of Christendome . . .' During the seventeenth century, to the buildings described by Coryat, Baldassare Longhena after the great plague of 1630 added the last great architectural component, in the style of the baroque, principally with the Church of Santa Maria della Salute. Coryat described the city as it stood before this final perfecting – Gothic and Byzantine, Renaissance and Neo-Classical – and in some animated passages brought the scene to life with the movement and voices of the patricians and the people.

On July the tenth, he saw the commemoration at the Church of the Redentore of Venice's relief from the plague of 1576. Over a bridge of boats stretching to Giudecca, almost a mile long, 'I observed an exceeding multitude of people flocking together to that Church, and passing forth and backe over the bridge . . . That day I saw a marvailous solemne Procession. For every Order and Fraternity of religious men in the whole city met together, and carried their Crosses and candlesticks of silver in procession to the Redeemers Church, and so backe againe to their severall Convents. Besides there was much good fellowship in many places of Venice upon that day. For there were many places, whereof each yeelded allowance of variety of wine and cakes and some other prety junkats to a hundred good fellowes to be merry that day . . .'

Coryat tried his rusty 'olde Greeke' on the Bishop Gabriel of Philadelphia, in the Greek Church (San Giorgio dei Greci) and found that he spoke the purest and most elegant Greek he had ever heard. The Greeks whom Coryat met were 'very blacke' and wore long hair, 'a fashion unseemly and very ruffian-like'.

In a Venetian play-house, Coryat witnessed women acting – which he had never before seen though he had heard of it

The Pope honours the Doge

occurring in London – and a bevy of courtesans, carefully disguised: 'they wore double maskes upon their faces . . . Upon their heads they wore little blacke felt caps . . . Also each of them wore a black short Taffeta cloake.' The courtesans sat high up in the play-house in the best room; if any man tried to unmask them, even in merriment, 'he should be cut to pieces before he should come forth of the roome, especially if he were a stranger.'

The Doge, Coryat saw on his way to St Mark's, accompanied by senators in long-sleeved gowns of damask and by knights and ambassadors. The Doge himself wore two rich robes, the uppermost of cloth of silver, with massy buttons of gold, the other also cloth of silver adorned with 'curious workes made in colours with needle-worke'.

In St Mark's, Coryat enjoyed the 'best musicke that ever I did in all my life'. He heard a treble viol, sackbuts and cornets; and in one of the halls of the religious companies, choirs and musicians performing so as to transport him into the third heaven.

He heard a soloist, who might have been a eunuch, singing 'sweeter than a nightingale'.

The gentlemen of Venice, who numbered about three thousand, he saw going about their business in their gowns of black cloth, after the style of the Roman toga; he observed their extraordinary habit when two of them met or parted of giving a mutual kiss on the cheek. The women usually wore long veils but they too caused him surprise, since they walked about with their breasts bare, and many of them with their backs naked as well. This seemed to Coryat an uncivil and unseemly business. 'For I beleeve unto many that have prurientem libidinem, they would minister a great incentive and fomentation of luxurious desires.'

Venetian women also, he noticed, wore 'chapineys' under their shoes, to increase their height; when walking abroad, they had to be supported by others.

And Coryat saw in Venice two men tormented by the strappado on St Mark's Square. After they were hoisted by rope, their limbs were loosed and pulled asunder, their faces flushed red with blood.

Coryat shook his head in disapproval not at such spectacles but at instances of unseemly dress and behaviour and of Popish superstition. He tut-tutted over the picture of Our Lady, allegedly painted by St Luke, which could cause rain to fall when carried in procession. Throughout his very thorough report however, admiration as well as wonder runs as the main thread. He lauds the status of the gentlemen of Venice, which kings had aspired to obtain; remarks their great wealth and yet their frugality, which is enforced by edict; and above all, he commends the historical inviolability of their city, with its mixed constitution and glorious empire on land and overseas.

Venice was privileged above all cities, thrice-fortunate and thrice-blessed, because she had been preserved intact from all invasions; despite all attempts to deflower her, she remained 'a mayden city . . . with her virginity untouched'.

Coryat possessed a knowing eye for the picturesque and for the kind of lively everyday detail that often escapes the historian. He registers the innocent gaiety and soft corruptions of Venice in marvellous pictorial reporting and comment, which also unselfconsciously reflect the preoccupations of contemporary

Englishmen. Coryat particularly illuminated, in this double mirror, the nature of Venice's appeal to the English political thinker as well as to the merely curious traveller. He distils the myth of Venice at a critical stage of its formation.

Through the 'liquid streets' of Venice, Coryat was conducted by the English ambassador, Sir Henry Wotton, and we must see the experiences and prejudice of Wotton in his perceptive observations on Venice's political structures and strength. The insight is often indirectly provided by a splash of gossipy detail, as when we are informed of Coryat's wonder, among the Venetians, 'that their Gentlemen and greatest Senators, a man worth perhaps two millions of duckats, will come into the market, and buy their flesh, fruites, and such other things as are necessary for the maintenance of their family . . .'

Coryat disapproved of this lack of gentlemanly behaviour, just as Castiglione would have done, but it points to a relaxed social relationship between Venice's immigrants and citizens (if not the slaves) and the three thousand 'Clarissimoes'.

Coryat wanted to give his English reader a 'superficial touch' regarding the government of Venice: 'I am neither polititian, nor statist, but a private man,' he protested. But he described the essentials of the still evolving constitution briefly and knowingly.

'The Duke is not a sovereigne Prince, to say *sic volo, sic jubeo* . . . the governement of this City is a compounded forme of state, contayning in it an Idea of the three principall governements of the auncient Athenians and Romans, namely the Monarchicall, the Oligarchicall, and Democraticall . . . Next is the Councell of ten commonly called Consilio di dieci . . . These are as it were the maine sinewes and strength of the whole Venetian Empire. For they are the principall Lordes of the state . . . The last is the great Councell which consisteth of a thousand and six hundred Gentlemen, who are likewise other subordinate members of the State . . .'

The idea of Venice's independence, inviolability, mystical secularism, and constitutional balance helped to shape European political thought during the Enlightenment. Coryat's interesting sexual imagery is repeated by another English visitor, the writer James Howell, who went to Venice to look at the glass business in 1618, and later wrote about Venice's 'dainty smooth neat

John Milton

Streets, whereon you may walk most days in the year in a Silk Stockin and Sattin-Slippers, without soiling them . . .'

Venice, Howell enthused, was a beauteous Maid: 'some have *courted* her, some *bribed* her, some would have *forc'd* her, yet she hath still preserv'd her Chastity entire . . .'

We shall meet the metaphor again after the rape of Venice by Napoleon, in Wordsworth's sonnet.

Sir Henry Wotton, a man of Kent, educated at Winchester and Oxford and the Middle Temple, agent and secretary to the Earl of Essex, acted as ambassador to Venice at intervals during the years 1604 to 1624. His whole career, ending with the Provost-ship of Eton, was intricately bound in with diplomacy, intelligence work, espionage. He knew intimately the European courts. It was he who wrote (in less ambiguous Latin) that an ambassador was an 'honest man sent to lie abroad for the good of his country'. He was a friend of John Donne and Isaac Walton and wrote some exquisite verse.

To Wotton, Coryat had a slightly mocking letter of introduction from Richard Martin, of the Middle Temple. Wotton's house in Venice was near the Ghetto (originally the spot for a foundry – *ghetto* in old Venetian – where Jewish migrants from the mainland were settled during the war of the League of Cambrai). Here, near S. Gerolamo ('in the streete called S. Hieronimo') Coryat saw Venice's Jews (five or six thousand of them, he believed) wearing yellow turbans if they were Levantine, and red hats if they were Western, and among them some few 'most elegant and sweet-featured persons'. In Wotton's street, Coryat also remarked, where the ambassador kept a Divine to ensure Protestant service and sermons in the midst of Popery and Idolatry, lived the famous Friar Paul of the Servite Order.

Coryat's reference to Paulo Sarpi touches just lightly on one of the great dramas of Venetian history. 'I mention him,' he wrote, 'because in the time of the difference betwixt the Signiory of Venice and the Pope, he did in some sort oppose himselfe against the Pope, especially concerning his supremacy in civill matters, and as wel with his tongue as his pen inveighed not a little against him. So that for his bouldnesse with the Popes Holynesse he was like to be slaine by some of the Papists in Venice, whereof one did very dangerously wound him. It is thought that he doth dissent in many points from the Papisticall doctrine, and inclineth to the Protestants religion, by reason that some learned Protestants have by their conversation with him in his Convent something diverted him from Popery . . .'

Sarpi's name brings with it the reminders of violence. The attempted assassination mentioned by Coryat left him near to death, a dagger thrust into his face. It was near to where a previous English ambassador, Harwell, in revenge for a slight had the elderly Pietro Aretino beaten with cudgels about half a century previously. But the violence was painted on a vaster canvas than the perennial street brawls of Venice. Sarpi, a versatile scholar and intellectual, and probably the profoundest, certainly the most influential of the few important philosophers born in Venice, began his career in an Augustinian convent, came to know the great Catholic reformer Cardinal Borromeo in Milan, worked in close contact with the Curia in Rome, and was appointed, for his usefulness and brilliance, the official theologian of the Venetian Republic.

He stands somewhat enigmatically in the spotlight of history, a figure enriching the mythology of Venice, as the champion of

Venetian naval squadron

national tradition and independence against the institutional 'violence' of the Counter-Reformation Papacy which was pitched against the determination of Venice to survive with its rights as a state intact, its sovereignty absolute.

In a portrait of him, a black patch on his cheek covers where the dagger struck.

The Papacy's quarrel with Venice sprang partly from the campaign, after the Council of Trent, to win back Papal authority over states seduced or threatened by nationalism and Protestantism; partly from the older struggle within the Catholic world between the rival claims of Church and State in ecclesiastical affairs; partly from the compulsion of two forceful leaders – Pope Paul IV and Doge Leonardo Doria – to assert themselves on behalf of the causes for which they had been elected. The Interdict of 1606 in general terms excluded the Catholic faithful from the celebration of their religious rites. It was Rome's dramatic riposte to the assertion by the Venetian state of its right to try ecclesiastics in secular courts, and throughout all Venetian territory to control the foundation of churches and the acquisition of property by churchmen.

Sarpi, as relentless and prolific a scholar as Machiavelli, shared the Florentine's intellectual guile and demonstrated more than his practical political cunning. He led the ideological battle against the Papacy with a success that extended beyond the frontiers of Venice when the Pope virtually caved in on the points at issue between Rome and Venice, though a face-saving formula was found for peace. Sarpi's writings – from the memorandum he wrote for the Senate to his influential *History of the Council of Trent* (first printed in London in 1619) – widely translated and admired outside Italy, documented for an eager audience the historical uniqueness of Venice, and the relevance of Venetian independence and sovereignty to the new aspirations of secular Europe. A bevy of other Venetian writers – notably Gasparo Contarini and Paolo Paruta – sustained his arguments. Venice was politically wise, it was concluded, above all because Venice survived, in an age when few European states had yet been safely formed and the oldest, France and England, were scarcely secure from internal disruption, foreign invasion or religious challenge to their sovereignty.

Venice survived also the continuing harassment of the Ottoman Empire, and not only through deals and compromise. The epic struggle against the Turk, continued in successive wars till the early eighteenth century, added lustre to the name of Venice and demonstrated the continuance of naval genius and of the capacity of the state's rulers to organise and lead, and to inspire military resourcefulness and courage.

The customary interpretation of Venetian history – the insistence on remorseless decline – seizes on the economic recession of the first part of the seventeenth century, on the exodus of the upper-classes into manufacture, farming and country-life pursuits away from global trading, sea-faring and civic involvement, on the exaltation of neutrality and peace as aims of state policy and on the collapse of attempts to widen the base of political power.

Otherwise coloured, those same years yield evidence of Venice's continuing energies in the ability of the government to act decisively, to lash out in the fight for survival, to seize the main chance, and to implement strategies of sound defence, calculated aggression and long-term survival.

Polemics and diplomacy were successful weapons against the Papacy. A decade after the Interdict, provoked by Venice's meddling neutrality, Spanish interests plotted to invade Venice from Naples, destroy the centres of political and military power – the Doge's Palace and the Arsenal – and install a Spanish puppet government. French mercenaries were gathered within Venice, hired by the Venetians but potential looters on the side of Venice's enemies. The plot was discovered. The Council of Ten gave a brutal sign of inner resolution by hanging the corpses of three of the conspirators from a gibbet on the Piazzetta. Then, simply asking the King of Spain to take back his ambassador, it stayed diplomatically and devastatingly silent about the whole affair.

The silence was profound in a mist of fear and conjecture rising over the lagoon. From the day of the revelation of a conspiracy – chilling people's blood in a Europe febrile with plots, counter-plots and assassinations – to the present time, all manner of theories have been propounded as to the nature of a Spanish conspiracy, including the supposition that it was invented. In discussing them, the robust, sometimes fanciful historian of Venice, Horatio Brown, British Consul in the nineteenth century, draws from the episode yet another moral of Venice's decline and decadence, the fresh myth that started to take shape in the eighteenth century as Venice seemed increasingly pleasure-loving and politically impotent – yet still survived.

Silence about Venice can be as profound as the silence of Venice itself. Not quite on the same exalted level as, but comparable to, the discovery of a letter by Dante or a missing sonnet by Shakespeare is what was not said by John Milton, sojourner in Venice in 1638. He had just published *Lycidas*. In his *Second Defence of the English People* (which first appeared in 1654), he recalled that after the death of his mother, he was curious to see foreign countries, and above all Italy. After obtaining his father's permission, he set out attended by one servant. 'On my departure,' he recalls, 'I was treated in the most friendly manner by Sir Henry Wotton, who was long ambassador from King James to Venice, and who not only followed me with his good wishes, but communicated, in an elegant letter, some maxims of the greatest use to one who is going abroad.' The consequences of Milton's Italian tour – to Genoa, Florence, Rome, Ferrara and Venice – remain for ever in his poetry and its influence. About Venice, he said little himself. Like Erasmus, another bookish man, he left nothing on record about his feelings concerning the beauty of the city. His biographer and nephew, Edward Phillips, writing about Milton in 1694, records that his uncle passed through *Bononia* and *Ferrara* to Venice 'where when he had spent a Month's time in viewing of that Stately City, and Shipp'd up a Parcel of curious and rare Books which he had pick'd up in his

Travels; particularly a Chest or two of choice Musick-books of the best Masters flourishing about that time in *Italy*, namely, *Luca Marenzo, Monte Verde, Horatio Vecchi, Cifa*, the *Prince of Verona* and several others, he took his course through *Verona, Milan*, and the *Poenine Alps*, and so by the Lake *Leman* to Geneva . . .'

During the early years of the century, Venice was tormented by the piracy of Christian corsairs in the Adriatic and the Mediterranean and by the arrogant presence of Spanish naval power. Then Spain was enfeebled by wars with the Dutch and the French. Pirates continued to attack Venetian shipping from the Barbary states. But the Ottoman Empire was the longest-lasting and most formidable threat to the survival of Venetian power at sea and on land.

Since Lepanto, under a succession of generally ineffective and sometimes unspeakable rulers, the Turkish empire had barely survived intact through bloodthirsty internal oppression and aggressive drives against Persia and in Europe. Communications by sea were vital, and here the main irritant to Ottoman zeal and security was the old partner and enemy, Venice. Under the

Venetian flag remained the Ionian Islands and Crete, which had been sold to Venice by Boniface of Monferrato (for a thousand silver marks) after the Fourth Crusade. Crete, a thriving centre of Greek art and learning and Orthodox religious observances since the fall of Constantinople, was a noble possession, more of symbolic than economic value to Venice, a desirable (but subsequently grossly ill-used) prize for the Turks.

The Knights of St John, rulers of Malta, attacked a Turkish fleet and captured from it some members of the harem of Sultan Ibrahim. A Turkish armada was sent against Crete and war declared against Venice in 1644. The Venetian defence of Crete – the island was finally lost in 1669 – and the energy with which Venice mobilised and sustained the effort of three successive wars against the Turks won plaudits from the rest of Western Europe (more often than help – Cromwell, Lord Protector of England, refused aid because the country's financial interests would suffer from Turkish hostility in the Mediterranean) and ranged Venetian power with important historic effect in combat and propaganda on the side of Poles, Hungarians, Austrians and Russians in their resistance against the Turks. In 1700, the peace of Karlowitz marked the end of Turkey's thrusts of conquest into Europe. Venice, after another outburst of war, in 1718 ceded the Morea to Turkey but kept several strongholds in Dalmatia and Albania.

Throughout these last Turkish wars, the Venetian commanders acted aggressively and intelligently, and won several impressive naval victories, notably the battle of the Dardanelles in 1656. The defence of the fortress of Candia, in Crete, linked the Venetians directly with the mainland struggle against the Turk through inspiring them – as they sought revenge – to join the anti-Turkish coalition in the 1680s, after Austrians and Poles had repulsed the Turkish assault on Vienna.

John III Sobieski, King of Poland, led the Christian forces against the Turks under Kara Mustapha at Vienna, and himself rode with the Polish cavalry in the charge which brought victory. It is a pleasing thought that this not-so-pleasant king, the heir of a fabulous fortune and huge estates, was among the first of the Europeans to undertake a formal 'Grand Tour' as part of his education.

Sobieski's name ought to be engraved on the European heart

as its defender against the Turk. I remember hearing it on the lips of refugee Polish children singing their national anthem during World War II. It underlines, too, the peculiar geography of one's own, Western European, English, mental map of Venice. Imagine approaching Venice from the East, from Dalmatia or Persia or the Barbary coast, rather than along the Brenta or over the mountains from the North. Or seeing the Venetian empire through the eyes of a Turkish admiral, or a galley-slave, or one of the migrant Slavs, after whom, one is carefully reminded today, the Riva degli Schiavoni was named.

During the Interdict, the Jesuits were expelled from Venice, as being obstinate in their loyalty to the Papacy. They were re-admitted, in deference to the Pope, when Venice joined the alliance against the Turks. One consequence of their temporary absence was an increase in the theatres that opened during the years of the mid-century all over Venice. (Until recently at least, I recall from my schooldays, members of the Society of Jesus were allowed to go to the cinema freely, but must obtain permission from their superior to visit the theatre.) Whatever the influence of the Jesuits' expulsion, during the sixteenth century new sights and sounds enriched the cultural life of the city.

The Malibran was founded (in a part of Venice near the Rialto still thick with names and structures dating back to Marco Polo) in 1678. It was then called the Theatre of San Giovanni Crisotomo. The Theatre of San Samuele, also under the patronage of the Grimani family, was opened in 1665, and in the next century provided the first platform for the early plays of Carlo Goldoni. What is today the Goldoni theatre was opened under the name of San Luca by the Vendramin family early in the seventeeth century. The Teatro San Moisè, on the Grand Canal, which is now closed, opened in 1638 with a showing of Monteverdi's *L'Arianna*.

The vitality of the theatre in seventeenth-century Venice was a necessary factor in the miracle of serendipity which saw the growth, through its first completed phase of development, of the new, magical and influential art form of the Italian opera.

Theatre-going had been a passion of the Venetians since the beginning of the previous century. More than in other Italian cities, it provided popular entertainment. Aretino's four comedies – nothing as good was staged in this genre till Goldoni – and his one impressive classical tragedy, were published in the 1530s and 1540s. The Venetians' love of music and their multitude of churches (Coryat counted three hundred) and above all the combined sacral and secular importance of San Marco contributed other strands.

In Venice and elsewhere, the evolution of sacred plays and spectacles (Vasari's life of Brunelleschi provides an important description of their elaborate mechanical apparatus) helped the breakthrough from classical rigidities to the rich and elaborate presentations of the plays of Tasso and Ariosto. The pastoral drama – performed on stage with dancing and music – reached peaks of sophisticated elegance in Tasso's *Aminta* and Giovanni Battista Guarini's *Il Pastor Fido* in the late sixteenth century. And in Florence, in the 1590s, a group of writers and musicians (known as the *Camerata*), inspired by the humanist ambition to clarify and emulate ancient, classical models, sought to promote musical forms that gave primacy to the role of poetic declamation, to the words, in musical performances. They can be said to have given birth to opera; Venice gave it its cradle.

The first 'opera' – a series of compositions for a single voice, with an instrumental background – was *Dafne*, the classical tale of Apollo and Daphne. The music was by Jacopo Peri; the words by Ottavio Rinuccini, and it was first performed in Florence in 1594. Most of the very early operas were meant for performance at court, to delight and stimulate noble audiences. The genius of Monteverdi both revolutionised the form and significance of the opera within a few years of its invention, and also, through the accidents of his personal fortune, almost immediately concentrated its creatively explosive influence in Venice.

Monteverdi, enamelling words with music to fashion glittering dramas of intellect and passion, produced his first operas, the *Orfeo* and the *Arianna* for the court of Mantua, where he had been *maestro di cappella* to the Gonzagas since 1602. He was famous throughout Italy as a composer of motets and madrigals, and in 1610 appeared his excellent, bejewelled *Vespro della Beata Vergine*, whose technical virtuosity and sustained spiritual magnificence must have put beyond challenge his claim to the post of *maestro di cappella* at Venice in 1613, in succession to Giovanni Gabrieli.

Before his death in 1643, Monteverdi, both a brilliant exponent of traditional polyphonic forms and an inspired innovator in the

73

new forms of monody and *musica parlante*, composed a series of operas, including the masterpieces *Il Ritorno d'Ulisse in Patria* (1641) and supremely *L'Incoronazione di Poppea*, the subtle, sensuous, emotionally disturbing and musically dazzling crown to his career.

Pierfrancesco Cavalli, Monteverdi's pupil, inherited the public acclaim and musical resources with which Venice sustained Monteverdi's achievements, and widened the popular appeal of the opera through making it more humorous and accessible. When he went to Paris his operas were to disappoint the French, who followed another path of development, but their simplicity and lightness of touch (in *L'Ormindo* and *La Calisto*) have satisfied modern audiences.

Seventeen or more theatres had been opened in Venice by the end of the seventeenth century. Totting up the performances of opera that there must have been, the usually phlegmatic historian Frederic Lane exclaims: 'Imagine all that opera in a modern city with a population of only 140,000!'

Opera, the glory and often the solace of Venice in the seventeenth and eighteenth centuries, has been derided as well as loved since its beginnings. I have always been one of the enthusiasts. My interest was first aroused, as with many other pleasures, through the enticement of a particular human voice. The *bel canto* of Caruso; and then Chaliapin, McCormack, Tetrazzini, Melba, Galli-Curci, on 78 rpm records thick as tortoises' shells with plum, purple and blood-red labels, thrilled me when I was young and still do. Among the hostile critics of opera, for a reason, was Joseph Addison, whom we shall meet in Italy further on, and who said concerning the popularity of opera in London while Racine could be seen: 'Would one think it possible (at a time when an author lived that was able to write the *Phaedra and Hippolitus*) for a people to be so stupidly fond of the Italian opera, as scarce to give a third day's hearing to that admirable tragedy?'

The opera heard in eighteenth-century England was not, however, Monteverdi. His music has always been neglected in England, till recently. Now amends have been made. As John Higgins shows himself inclined to believe, in *The Making of an Opera*, 'Glyndebourne can take much of the credit for the baroque revival which has rolled across Western Europe and America . . .'

In the early 1970s, Glyndebourne moved from Italian comic opera to Monteverdi's *L'Incoronazione di Poppea* and *Il Ritorno*

74

d'Ulisse in Patria, and Cavalli's *La Calisto* and *L'Ormindo*. His three surviving operas were produced as a 'cycle' by the Zurich Opera at the Edinburgh Festival in 1978. During the writing of this chapter, thanks to the joyful surge of fresh interest in Monteverdi, I have been able to listen to recordings of some of his madrigals, two of his Masses, of *L'Orfeo*, of the *Vespers*, of *Poppea*. This is to traverse a musical universe of immense dimensions and contrasts, where paths range confidently from the sweet tones of medieval ascetism to the tumultuous richnesses of complex baroque.

In music, architecture, painting, sculpture, in the very air and atmosphere of Italy, manifestations of baroque waited in Rome, Naples, Venice for those seventeenth-century travellers to the south who were shaping the conventional itinerary of the *giro d'Italia*, the Grand Tour. As for centuries past, for visitors to Venice from Italy or abroad, it was *de rigueur* to arrange to be in Venice on the feast of the Ascension, forty days after Easter. John

The Commedia dell'Arte:
Trivelino and Scaramuccia

Evelyn was staring at the *Bucintoro*, being rowed along by St Mark's, in 1644, shortly after he had been to Rome and discovered opera.

Faint-hearted, philoprogenitive, prolific, a Balliol and Middle Temple man from Surrey, a dabbler in art criticism, a devoted civil servant, and an influential authority on trees and forests, Evelyn is important for what he observed during a long life stretching through the English civil wars and the Revolution against James II rather than for what he thought. His vast *Diary* covers most of his life.

First published in full only in 1955 (edited by E. S. de Beer) the volumes spill over with descriptions of great contemporaries and panoramic accounts of the towns and cities of Italy, France, Flanders and the Low Country.

In 1643, Evelyn set out to tour France and Italy. He landed after rough weather at Calais for Paris; voyaged by sea from Cannes to Genoa; went on to Pisa, Florence, Siena and Rome; visited Naples (where the best, most plentiful food was found), and the ruins of Cuma; and then, after returning to Rome, journeyed to Florence, Bologna, Ferrara and Venice, where he landed from the Adriatic at Malamocco.

Very appropriately in the context of the stupendous magnificence of St Peter's, Evelyn first mentions the 'opera' when recording his visit to Rome. The high altar of St Peter's, he writes, with its four great columns, pedestals, crown and statues, 'form a thing of that art, vastnesse, and magnificence, beyond all that ever man's industry has produced of this kind: it is the work of Bernini, a Florentine sculptor, architect, painter, and poet, who, a little before my coming to the City, gave a public Opera (for so they call shews of that kind) wherein he painted the scenes, cut the statues, invented the engines, compos'd the musiq, writ the comedy, and built the theatre. . . .'

Back in Rome after a journey further south, in the summer of 1645, Evelyn again mentions being present at an opera. 'We were entertain'd at Night with an English play, at the Jesuites where before we had dined, & the next at the Prince Galicanos, who himselfe compos'd the Musique to a magnificent Opera, where were Cardinal Pamphilio the Popes Nephew, the Governors of Rome, the Cardinals, Ambassadors, Ladies & a world of Nobilitie & strangers . . .'

Street scene: the Commedia dell'Arte

Next time he saw an opera Evelyn named and described it in fascinating detail and gave it the marvellous setting of a Venetian night. He was in the company of Lord Bruce, the second Earl of Elgin, whose son was to be imprisoned as a Jacobite. They went

'to the Opera, which are Comedies (& other plays) represented in Recitative Music by the most excellent Musitians vocal & Instrumental, together with variety of Seeanes painted & contrived with no lesse art of Perspective, and Machines, for flying in the aire, & other wonderfull motions. So taken together it is doubtlesse one of the most magnificent & expensfull diversions the Wit of Men can invent: The historie was *Hercules* in Lydia, the Seanes chang'd 13 times, The famous Voices *Anna Rencia* a Roman, & reputed the best treble of Women; but there was an *Eunuch*, that in my opinion surpass'd her, and a *Genoveze* that sung an incomparable Base: This held us by the Eyes and Eares til two in the Morning when we went to the *Chetto* de San: Felice, to see the Noblemen & their Ladies at *Basset*, a Game at Cards which much use, but play not in publique & with all that have inclination to it, in Masquerad . . .'

Evelyn found Venice, in 1645, under the rule of Doge Francesco Erizzo, about to embark on the bitterly fought and protracted defence of Crete, and proudly 'challenging the Empire of all the Adriatique Sea, which they yearly espouse, by casting a gold ring into it, with greate pomp & ceremony upon Ascention day . . .'

His eye for personality and movement presents us with a Venice that is solidly peopled and animated. He is as impressionable and naive as Coryat, telling again the story – just recounted to him by an eye-witness in the Piazza de San Marco – of 'the fellow who kept the Clock, struck with this hammer so forcably, as he was stooping his head neere the bell to mend something amisse, at the instant of striking, that being stunn'd, he reel'd over the battlements, & brake his neck.'

He is remarkably active, planning suddenly to go to the Holy Land, laying in snow on board ship to cool the drink and storing provisions, only to be frustrated by the Turks' attack on Candia for which reason the ship is impounded by the State. He bustles about the whole of Venice by night and day, admiring most of what he sees, save the dark and dismal interior of St Mark's.

A series of pictures flickering into colourful life shows us the Merceria, one of the most 'delicious' streets in the world, with its variegated hangings of gold, damasks and silks, its many shops, and 'the innumerable cages of Nightingals, which they keepe, that entertaines you with their melody from shop to shop, so as shutting your Eyes, you would imagine your selfe in the Country, when indeede you are in the middle of the Sea: besides there being neither rattling of Coaches nor trampling of horses, tis almost as silent as the field.'

Then after the square of St Mark's and the Basilica, the jealously guarded Treasure. Pure gold armour and crowns, caps set with rubies, vases of agate and unicorns' horns, heads of saints chased with gold and a profusion of extraordinary relics, are catalogued by Evelyn in what registers of tone it is not hard to imagine:

'In another part of this Treasurie we were shewed by a Priest (who first vested himselfe in his sacerdotals, with the Stola about his neck) the Evangelium of St Mark the Venetians Patron or Tutelarie, affirmed to be written by his owne hand, & whose Body (transported many yeares since from Alexandria) they shew buried in this Church: Also a small Ampulla or glasse of our B: Saviou(r)s blood, as they fancy: A greate morcell of the real Crosse, one of the nailes, a Thorne, a fragment of the Column to which our Lord was bound, when Scourged: The Labbarum or Ensigne (Standard) of victorious Constantine, a

78

Bull-baiting in the Piazza San Marco

piece of St Lukes arme, a rib of St Stephen, a finger of Mary Magdalene & a world of Reliques I could not remember.'

The ladies of Venice are still stepping out on their *choppines*, as Evelyn calls the high-heeled shoes, and not only are they *mezzo carne, mezzo ligno* but, because of the way they wear their petticoats from under the arm-pits, 'they are neere three quarters and a half apron . . .'

In the Arsenal, 'thought to be one of the best furnish'd in the world', walled about and with twelve towers for the watch, and environed by the sea, and employing about five hundred workmen, Evelyn sees the carpenters building oars and masts for a hundred galleys and ships, the saltpetre houses, the gun stores, the court with arms for 800,000 men and the 16,573 lbs cannon which was cast and put into a galley which was rigged and fitted for launching, all within the time that Henry III took to dine, on the occasion of his remarkable visit in 1574 to the Venice which then took the blame – it so much turned his head – for his subsequent decadent behaviour.

79

The frozen lagoon

Venice could still strive to be as outrageously frivolous and joyfully, conspicuously wasteful as when the King of France was there to entertain. Evelyn, returning to the city and its new Doge Francesco Molino from a sojourn at Padua in 1646, described the 'folly and madnesse' of the Carnival . . .

'The Women, Men & persons of all Conditions disguising themselves in antique dresses, & extravagant Musique & a thousand gambols, & traversing the streetes from house to house, all places being then accessible, & free to enter: There is abroad nothing but flinging of Eggs fill'd with sweete Waters, & sometimes not over sweete; they also have a barbarous costome of hunting bulls about the Streetes & Piazzas, which is very dangerous, the passages being generally so narrow in that Citty: Likewise do the youth of the severall Wards & parrishes contend in other Masteries or pastimes, so as tis altogether impossible to recount the universal madnesse of this place during this time of licence: Now are the greate banks set up for those who will play at Basset, the Comedians have also liberty & the Operas to Exercise: Witty pasquils are likewise thrown about, & the Mountebanks have their stages in every Corner:'

But there is a dignified enviable role for John Evelyn to play, this Carnival time in Venice.

'The diversion which chiefly tooke me up, was three noble Operas which I saw, where was incomparable Voices & Musique: The most celebrated of which was the famous Anna Rencha, whom we invited to a Fishdinner, after 4 daies in Lent, that they had given over at the Theater; when accompanied with an Eunuch (whom she brought with her) she entertaind us with rare Musique, both of them singing to an Harpsichord: It growing late a Gentleman of Venice came for her, to shew her the Gallys now ready to set sayle for Candia:'

I would leave Evelyn there, with the sound of music and the sea and the fragrance lingering of the great operatic singer from Rome. But there is another image which reminds us of the balance of Venice between sea and land, describing the journey between the lagoon and Padua that cannot be made without the sense of how we live in different ages all the time.

Evelyn was going, in June, to see the Fair of St Anthony at Padua.

'The first *Terra firma* we landed at was Fusina, being onley an Inn, where we changed our Barge, & were then drawne up with horses through the *River Brenta*, a strait Channell, as even as a line for 20 miles, the Country on both sides deliciously planted with Country Villas & gentlemens retirements, Gardens planted with Oranges, Figs, & other fruit, belonging to the *Venetians*. At one of these *Villas* we went on shore to see a pretty contrivd Palace: Observable in this passage was their buying their Water of those who farme the sluces, for this artificial river is in some places so shallow, that reserves of water are kept with sluces, which they open & shut with a most ingenious invention or Engine, so as to be governd even by a child: Thus they keep up the water, or dismisse it, till the next channell be either filled by the stop, or abated to the levell of the other; for which every boate pays a certaine dutie: Thus we stayed neere halfe an houre, & more at 3 severall interruptions, so as it was evening ere we got to Padoa.'

Evelyn never knew the word but the style of the Venice he observed and of the Rome to which it was culturally linked was the baroque. Not quite a weasel word, it has in the past implied some sort of decadence, colouring our image of the seventeenth century as a whole. It has no frontier in time and its usage is often as arbitrary as the historians' division of a nation's life into centuries. And another truer aspect of the baroque, which can be best defined by the single works of art classified under its name, is energy.

In his book on *Civilisation*, Kenneth Clark associates the work of Claudio Monteverdi with that of his younger contemporary, Gianlorenzo Bernini. Discussing the statue of the *Ecstasy of St Theresa*, he finds in Bernini's visual art and in Monteverdi's music a combination of 'deep feeling, sensuous involvement and marvellous technical control'. Art, Lord Clark muses, escaped 'from reality into a world of illusion'. In Venice, with the arrival of Monteverdi from Mantua, we enter the world running parallel in time with the reality of the Turkish wars and the domination by foreigners of Italy of this alleged illusionism of baroque.

Exploitation also, considers Lord Clark, was a feature of the baroque. For example, 'the colossal palaces of the Papal families were simply expressions of private greed and vanity . . . The sense of grandeur is no doubt a human instinct, but, carried too far, it becomes inhuman.'

Yet the energy is undeniable, an integral part of the baroque. In the aerial ballets over one's head in the Churches of the Gesu and St Ignazio, the Palazzo Barberini (again I quote Lord Clark): 'We feel that the stopper is out. Imaginative energy is fizzing away, up into the clouds, and will soon evaporate.'

However that may be, if the energy of the baroque is fundamental, so too is the religious faith that inspired it. In their *Dictionary of Art and Artists*, Peter and Linda Murray remark that in baroque the 'blend of illusionism, light and colour, and movement is calculated to overwhelm the spectator by a direct emotional appeal'. Then they give the warning that: 'Owing to its essential links with Counter-Reformation Catholicism, pagan antiquity, and the Mediterranean generally, many Northerners are – or were until recently – queasy about it . . .'

And not only Northerners. Venice, like the baroque style which its artists and musicians assimilated and extended, is a whirlpool of Catholicism, paganism, Mediterranean softness and mist, and hot Latin energy. In the seventeenth century, its religious impulses pitched materialism and triumphalism against spirituality and quietism; it tried to balance them.

Even today, one senses a continuing struggle. I remember Albino Luciani (a priest from the mountains in the north), soon to be elected Pope John Paul I, talking to me gently in the Patriarchical Palace about the materialism of the Venetians: about what was signified by the treasures of St Mark.

But the Venetians listened avidly in the Basilica of St Mark's to the baroque music of Monteverdi which cannot be explored only in terms of sensuality and imaginative energy but must be seen equally as the affirmation of hope: the unceasing striving to bring down the other-worldly vision of salvation to the present human stage. To triumph in glory here and now.

As a triumphant worldly witness to the glory of the world to come, the Church of Santa Maria della Salute rivals the music of Monteverdi. Like Monteverdi's Mass of 1631, it was an act of thanksgiving for Venice's deliverance from the plague of 1630, when over 46,000 Venetians died. It was, in architecture, the most opulent and enduring expression of Venice's adaptation of the baroque, commissioned by the State from Baldassare Longhena, a young native-born Venetian. Building was well underway when Evelyn landed at the nearby customs-point, the Dogana, in 1645, but not completed till 1686, three years after Longhena's death. The domed octagonal church was and is the most conspicuous in Venice, dominating the skyline on the far side of the Giudecca canal. Ruskin, in *The Stones of Venice*, cited its colossal scale (its dome the principal one by which Venice is first discerned, 'rising out of the distant sea') in comparison with the modest size of Palladio's Redentore to measure the 'relative importance of the ideas of the Madonna and of Christ, in the modern Italian mind'.

On its unique site, with its two domes and belfries, its chapels clustered below and the great doorway arch, massy and gleaming, the church dedicated to Our Lady unifies the view of the Giudecca from across the water and has become an unforgettable part of Venice's image, in reality and in recall. Longhena also dropped into place two smaller but precious parts of this Venetian mosaic: the Ca' Pesaro and (as it is now called) the Ca' Rezzonico (finished in the next century) where Browning died. These beautiful palaces record the intricate influences at work in the culture of seventeenth-century Venice, the pride of Doges and patricians, the skill of the craftsmen, the values, combining ostentation and civic pride, to which they subscribed.

I find very little written about seventeenth-century Venice which is not grudging in its praise or replete with damning hindsight. If this is justified, we can savour all the more the irony in Evelyn's last brief note on subjects Venetian: his comment in

Ca' Rezzonico

1696 that, in London, 'The Venetian Ambassador made a stately entry, with 50 footmen, many on horseback, 4 rich coaches, and a numerous train of gallants . . .'

But Venetian ambassadors have another hundred years of existence, and the eighteenth century in its turn will reveal once again the vitality of Venice – indeed an extraordinary renascence of the arts – before the end of its existence as an independent state. Frederic C. Lane's chapter on 'The Death of the Republic' in his *Venice* sets the scene:

'For almost eighty years, from 1718 to 1797, while Europe's great powers were engaged in major wars, Venice enjoyed peace (except for actions against pirates). One might expect that Venetian statesmen would be praised for this avoiding the horror of war, especially in light of what Venice produced during those years in music, literature, and the fine arts . . .'

4 *Pains and Pleasures: the Shattered Glass*

'Venetians of the times called themselves decadent,' Lane continues, 'in that they were not doing what their forefathers had done. Modern historians call them decadent because they were so much concerned with doing what their ancestors had done, and because they did not build new institutions contributing to the making of the future Italian nation.'

If there are parallels to be drawn between Venetian and English history, Lane provides the text and the eighteenth century the illustrations. Future historians may criticise the twentieth-century English for not building new institutions. They may ask whether the English were really showing the rest of the world how to live. They will analyse the reasons for their declining share of world trade and their slack response to the loss of empire. They will ponder the continuance in several areas (fiction, the performing arts, aerospace) of technical and creative excellence; the decay of dogmatic religion; the exile of talent; the ill-repute abroad for treachery and dissoluteness; the closed system of government; the co-existence of social tolerance and civic ruthlessness; the passion and aptitude for ceremony; and the pursuit of easy pleasure.

The giving and taking of pleasure seemed the very purpose of life in eighteenth-century Venice. It both stimulated and was stimulated by the swelling numbers of foreigners who visited and often settled in Venetian territory. The Grand Tour renewed the sources of patronage. The pleasures and the internationalism of Venice encouraged an astonishing artistic renewal embracing the opera, the theatre, and painting. The glittering physical image of eighteenth-century Venice shining through the crystal-thin deposits of time; the images formed in Venetian minds about their own sensually relaxed city, and the images caught and committed to posterity by travellers to Venice in the last years of its inviolate independence: all of them convey pleasure as the principal constituent of the Serenissima's life.

Pleasure was the *leitmotiv* in the drama of eighteenth-century

Tiepolo's Cosmorama (detail)

Venice but not the single theme. Artists sought to please, but also observed the prosaic and the painful behind the surface joyfulness and serenity of Venetian life.

During the first half of the century, religious themes still predominated in the airily colourful and delicately exultant decorative paintings of Sebastiano Ricci, G. A. Pellegrini, and Jacopo Amigoni, who travelled the courts of Europe, and in the work of G. B. Piazzetta, whose rich intensity of feeling cuts decisively across the impression of an irreligiously corrupt Venice. Still pursuing religious themes, influenced by the prettiness and intricacy of French rococo, Tiepolo, born in Venice, developed a strong personal style, which could embody dizzy perspectives, swirling figures and rich colours on a vast, apparently effortlessly controlled scale. His main works were done for the Archbishop's Palace at Udine, the Palazzo Labia at Venice, and the Prince-Bishop's Residenz at Wurzburg (1750–53) where he and his assistants created a huge allegorical masterpiece, stunningly appropriate to the rococo architecture, and teetering on the edge of the absurdity of which he was later to be accused.

In all these paintings of light and air and intense colour, charmingly pastoral, religious, allegorical, there was a mood of exuberant, sometimes frivolous, virtuosity. Illusionism, especially in the frescoes of Tiepolo, was complete, with distance, light and air suspended before the eyes of the spectator in compositions as convincing as reflections in still, clear water.

Creating its own kind of illusions, and perpetuating them as images of Venice for the future, was the realism of the great view-painters, the *vedutisti*, contemporary with Tiepolo, of whom the finest were Canaletto (1697–1768) and Francesco Guardi (1712–1793). Both benefited from the wealthy patronage of the English, among whom was the remarkable Joseph Smith, British Consul at Venice from 1744, whose large personal collection of pictures was bought in 1762 for King George III to become a permanent part of the Royal Collection, creating a lasting intimacy between English taste and Venetian art of the eighteenth century. Both too rescue Venetian painting from allegations of frivolousness and decay.

Canaletto, who visited England at least three times, fixed in the imaginations of thousands the classical set pieces of the Venetian landscape in which idealised, sharply detailed buildings rise from broad stretches of shining canal and courtyard into luminous blue skies. As his work evolved from earlier renderings of light and shade to the portrayal of open space drenched in light, his technique presented surfaces of paint of exquisite flawlessness. It was artificial, laboured, yet he rendered the truth: of Venice imagined, of Venice remembered in the tranquillity of the mind's eye and of Venice actually seen at a precise moment of a particular combination of tones of water, land, air. And if you look carefully at his pictures, as Michael Levey has pointed out in a vehement defence of Canaletto as 'the Respecter of Facts' (in a lecture at the National Gallery in 1978) you find a loving, detailed and historically accurate record of the day-to-day life of Venice counterpointing the important State occasions and the official monuments: it is all life unfolding. It is Venice at work.

Guardi, too, still more profoundly, points beyond the surfaces of Venetian life to the troubled depths of contemporary sensibilities. His views of Venice – drawings and paintings showing the processions of the Doge, scenes on the Grand Canal, the Lagoon frozen over – capturing historical events, nonetheless create an elusive atmosphere of mystery and nostalgia, using almost impressionistic techniques that dissolve time and space. He died within four years of the fall of the Republic, poorer and far less fashionable than Canaletto. He can still disturb the heart.

One of Guardi's paintings (in the Kaiser Friedrich Museum, Berlin) shows the ascent of a balloon at Venice. The date was 14 April, 1784. The balloon took off almost opposite the piazzetta of San Marco, on the Grand Canal, piloted by Count Francesco Zambeccari. This was about five months after Zambeccari launched a silk balloon filled with hydrogen from the Artillery ground in London; and just under a year after the Montgolfiers first publicly sent a balloon into the air in France. We see the back of cloaked Venetians standing under immensely tall pillars staring into the sky: dignity struggling with curiosity; haunting 'types' of Venice.

A large proportion of the paintings by Venetian artists of the *settecento* were either executed abroad or marked for export. For their own city, the painters' most notable work included the restoration of past glories. In the Doge's Palace, a restoration centre was established. Canvases by Titian, Tintoretto and Veronese were repaired. Tiepolo replaced a damaged Tintoretto with his *Neptune*.

While Venetian painting sought international markets abroad and was stimulated by the patronage of upper-class tourists, Venetian music, especially the opera, also bounded into unprecedented popularity at home. Baldassare Galuppi (1706–85), from Murano, was appointed San Marco's *maestro di cappella* in 1762, by when he had written a series of melodious comic operas, in many cases using libretti by the equally popular Goldoni. The *opera buffa* suited the Venetians' taste for ribaldry, sentimentality and gaiety. But their passion for music touched deeper levels. Galuppi was in London between 1741 and 1744 and influenced English musical taste and composition. (A century later, his name inspired Browning's *Toccato of Galuppi's* in which eighteenth- century Venice inspired the phrase 'when the kissing had to stop'.) Galuppi also wrote masses, oratorios and *concerti*, which were then beginning their evolution in Venice towards the form of the concertos of Bach and Mozart. His compositions were among the lighter contributions to the totality of Venetian music which embraced the enduring rediscovered works of Antonio Vivaldi and Tomaso Albinoni.

Pleasure, of course, is what the Venetians, and what we today, seek and find in Vivaldi's *The Seasons* or in Albinoni's *Adagio*. Their sheer output – Vivaldi over four hundred concertos and forty operas, Albinoni about a hundred concertos and fifty operas – points to the seriousness of the reception of music in Venice (though Vivaldi died impoverished in Vienna) as do the strength and prestige of the musical institutions of the city's four *ospedali*. Like the names of Canaletto and Guardi, those of Vivaldi and Albinoni are tokens of the richness of the continuation of Venice's artistic and musical genius in the eighteenth century. Listening as well as looking reveals strains of melancholy, some extreme and exquisite sadness, alongside the lightness and joy.

So did the tourists flock to Venice just for pleasure? Riding South, in the eighteenth century, mostly from England and mostly on the Grand Tour, they included the young nobleman, set to improve his mind, his tutor, to keep an eye on him, the scholar or intellectual, in search of knowledge on his own account, and in increasing numbers, the prosperous middle-aged man or woman catching the habit and seeking cultural experience or recreation. Professor Robert Shackleton, erstwhile Bodley's Librarian and a lover of Italy no less than of France, remarks in a paper on *The Grand Tour in the Eighteenth Century* that: 'Venice was not, in the eighteenth century, the most intellectually active city in the peninsular, but it retained the memory, sometimes fading, of great traditions . . .'

Professor Shackleton notes the disparagement of Venice by Montesquieu in 1728, when he suggested that its much-vaunted liberty was simply licence.* But pleasures of all sorts abounding in the city attracted other, not always less intellectually austere, tourists, in increasing numbers during the eighteenth century; drew gratified praise from many when they left, and from the good number who settled and, ironically, fed the fires of moralising satisfaction still flickering today over Venice's collapse.

* '*Quant à la liberté,*' said Montesquieu, '*on y jouit d'une liberté que la plupart des honnêtes gens ne veulent pas avoir: aller de plein jour voir des filles de joie; se marier avec elles; pouvoir ne pas faire ses pâques; être entièrement inconnu et indépendant dans ses actions: voilà la liberté que l'on a*'.
['As for liberty, there one enjoys the kind of liberty most decent people do not want to have: to visit the girls of the town in broad daylight; to marry them; not to have to make one's Easter duties; to be entirely unrecognised and independent in one's deeds: there's the liberty that one has'].

The Venetians themselves, in the days of the Grand Tour, laughed with some self-satisfaction at their own life-style; kept their pride in the Venetian state; but generally, when they dared, lambasted their rulers.

The preposterous Casanova is a witness for the prosecution whom Montesquieu would have felt it a defilement to call. I have the twelve volumes of Arthur Machen's translation from the French of the 1922 Casanova Society edition ('privately printed for subscribers only') in front of me as I write. 'The chief business of my life has always been to indulge my senses; I never knew anything of greater importance,' wrote the most notorious of all Venetians. But as well as turning up the sodden underside of the pleasures of Venetian life, he paints unforgettable pictures of ordinary public and private life that have become extraordinarily exotic at this distance of time. His 'audacious hand' can charm as well as shock us as much as it did the women he seduced.

Casanova, writing at the end of the eighteenth century about Venice in mid-century, adds to a description by Goldoni his account of the sweetness of a journey from Venice to Padua by the *burchiello*, a boat related to the gondola. The *burchiello*, he said, may be considered a small, floating house. 'There is a large saloon with a smaller cabin at each end, and rooms for servants fore and aft. It is a long square with a roof, and cut on each side by glazed windows with shutters. The voyage takes eight hours . . .' Goldoni records in his memoirs that at nightfall, as the *burchiello* moved gently through the water, the passengers, with oboes, violins, a French horn and a guitar, played music together in the open air. Casanova reminds of the fact that slaves as well as servants helped to provide the comforts – and it was believed ensure the safety – of middle and upper-class Venetian society.

He is philosophising as he looks back to his period of military service as a young man, when he was sent to Corfu, and then returned to Venice in a galleass. This vessel needed five hundred slaves to row it in a windless day and was expensive to maintain. The Venetian galleasses were put aside about that time, Casanova recalls, but only after long debate in the senate:

'and those who opposed the measure took their principal ground of opposition in the necessity of respecting and conserving all the institutions of olden times . . .

'That ground of opposition to all improvements, however absurd it may be, is a very powerful one in a republic, which must tremble at the mere idea of novelty either in important or in trifling things. Superstition has likewise a great part to play in these conservative views.

'There is one thing that the Republic of *Venice* will never alter: I mean the galleys, because the Venetians truly require such vessels to ply, in all weathers and in spite of the frequent calms, in a narrow sea, and because they would not know what to do with the men sentenced to hard labour.

'I have observed a singular thing in *Corfu*, where are often as many as three thousand galley slaves; it is that the men who row in the galleys, in consequence of a sentence passed upon them for some crime, are held in a kind of opprobium, while those who are there voluntarily are, to some extent, respected. I have always thought it ought to be the reverse, because misfortune, whatever it may be, ought to inspire some sort of respect; but the vile fellow who condemns himself voluntarily and as a trade to the position of a slave seems to me contemptible in the highest degree. The convicts of the Republic, however, enjoy many privileges, and are, in every way, better treated than the soldiers. It very often occurs that soldiers desert and give themselves up to a *sopracomito* to become galley slaves. In those cases, the captain who loses a soldier has nothing to do but to submit patiently, for he would claim the man in vain. The reason of it is that the Republic has always believed galley slaves more necessary than soldiers. The Venetian may perhaps now (I am writing these lines in the year 1797) begin to realise their mistake.'

During the carnival of 1745, Casanova, rambling through the streets of Venice with seven of his friends after midnight, all wearing masks, tricked three young men into handing over to them a beautiful young woman with whom they had been drinking in a wine-bar. After she had been seduced, the three men, one of whom was her husband, complained to the Council of Ten. The woman, Casanova claims, had not been unwilling. The Council of Ten offered a reward, but one of the eight was a noble Venetian belonging to the Balbi family. 'The rank of Balbi quieted my anxiety at once, because I knew that, even supposing one of us were vile enough to betray our secret for the sake of the reward,

93

the tribunal would have done nothing to implicate a patrician.'

Casanova's most animated and colourful images of Venice are in the scenes of night, when masked figures move under moonlight along the canals or through candle-lit rooms. On Twelfth Night, he has been in the early evening to gaze at Verrocchio's superb statue of the *condottiere* Colleoni by the Church of SS Giovanni e Paolo, known to the Venetians as San Zanipolo. And then: 'At six o'clock precisely my mistress alighted from the gondola, well dressed and well masked, by this time in the garb of a woman. We went to the *Saint Samuel* Opera, and after the second ballet we repaired to the *ridotto*, where she amused herself by looking at all the ladies of nobility who alone had the right to walk about without masks . . .'

Casanova's descriptions grow gradually sickly, heavy with grotesque escapades, with practical jokes reeking of cruelty rather than wit, and with deceits admiringly explained as if they constituted, like the mask and the adultery, the essential charm of Venice. At day-break on one occasion, not long before he was arrested on the orders of the State Inquisitors, he went to the *Erberia*, on the quay of the Grand Canal, where the herb, fruit and flower market was held.

'People in good society who come to walk in the *Erberia* at a rather early hour usually say that they come to see the hundreds of boats laden with vegetables, fruit and flowers, which hail from the numerous islands near the town; but everyone knows that they are men and women who have been spending the night in the excesses of *Venus* and *Bacchus*, or who have lost all hope at the gaming-table, and come here to breathe a purer air and to calm their minds. The fashion of walking in this place shows how the

Casanova

Regatta on the Grand Canal

character of a nation changes. The Venetians of old time who made as great a mystery of love as of state affairs, have been replaced by the modern Venetians, whose most prominent characteristic is to make a mystery of nothing. Those who come to the *Erberia* with women wish to excite the envy of their friends by this publishing their good fortune . . . the women come only to be seen, glad to let everybody know that they are without restraint upon their actions.'

He was telling the truth about the poor morals of the Venetians, Casanova said, as anyone could see just by going there.

Casanova most bitterly indicts Venice in the suspense-filled narration of his arrest (nominally for smuggling, perhaps for sorcery and suspected treason), imprisonment, and escape from the *piombi*, the prisons under the leads of the Doge's Palace.

'It is curious that in *London*, where everyone is brave, only one man is needed to arrest another, whereas in my dear native land, where cowardice prevails, thirty are required. The reason is, perhaps, that the coward on the offensive is more afraid than

95

the coward on the defensive, and thus a man usually cowardly is transformed for the moment into a man of courage. It is certain that at *Venice* one often sees a man defending himself against twenty *sbirri*,* and finally escaping after beating them soundly . . .'

After a journey along small canals to the *Canale Grande*, Casanova landed with his escort at the prison quay, crossed the notorious closed bridge between the Doge's Palace and the prisons (over the *Rio di Palazzo*) and then met the secretary of the Inquisitors 'who was apparently ashamed to speak Venetian in my presence as he pronounced my doom in the Tuscan language . . .'

The episode, ending with Casanova's elaborately recounted break-out from his cell, is reminiscent of Cellini's equally dramatic story of his adventurous flight from Castel Sant' Angelo. Casanova's sarcasm, self-justification, protestations of innocence, generally amoral register of voice and vivid imagination also match Cellini's, though he fails to achieve the Florentine's surrealist brilliance.

Like Casanova, the native playwrights Carlo Goldoni and Carlo Gozzi also depicted Venetian scenes of tremendous vitality but through their eyes the city sparkles with more charm, variety and humour, and exhibits a tremendous continuing pride in itself. They were vociferous rivals. Goldoni the innovator in the space of a decade wrote over sixty naturalistic comedies which shattered the traditional form of the *commedia dell'arte*, with its masked characters and extemporised dialogue. Gozzi, fighting back to preserve the old styles, fashioned influential new fantasies in his *fiabe* which included *Turandot* and *The Love of the Three Oranges*.

The writings of the two men, including their pugnacious memoirs, scatter paper-pictures of Venice and its citizens in genial profusion. Gozzi, a peppery, wickedly observant satirist, left home at twenty to become a volunteer soldier overseas. Years later, he remembered the appearance of a Venetian commander in those last days of empire.

'He made his appearance now in crimson – crimson mantle, cap and shoes – with an air of haughtiness unknown to me, and

* Police-runners of a ruffianly sort.

Bartolomeo Colleoni

fierceness stamped upon his features. The other officers informed me that when he donned this uniform of state, he had to be addressed with profound and silent salaams.'

Gozzi's recollections of his service in Dalmatia superimpose the scorn and glory of imperial Venice on the customary scenes of eighteenth-century revelry. The Slavs of Dalmatia, he wrote – the Morlacchi – were drafted at Zara for service in defence of Venice's neutrality at home.

'It is certain that the Italian cities under our benign government were now more disturbed than guarded by these brutal creatures. At Verona, in particular, they indulged their appetite for thieving, murdering, brawling, and defying discipline, without the least regard for others . . .

    'In the mountains the Morlacchi are fine fellows, useful to the State of Venice on occasions of war with the Turks, their neighbours, whom they cordially detest.'

But the main substance of Gozzi's memoirs is the domestic life of Venice at peace: a warm-hearted, crotchety, often tongue-in-cheek remembrance of love-affairs, of companies of actors, literary feuds and – at the end – of the fall of the Republic of Venice, viewed as a victim to insane and howling seekers after Liberty, Equality, Fraternity.

    'In spite of all the praise showered upon Goldoni,' said Gozzi, struggling as usual to be fair, 'paid for or gratis, by journalists, preface-writers, romancers, Voltaires, I do not think that, with the single exception of his *Beneficent Gambler* . . . he ever produced

97

a perfect dramatic piece. At the same time I must add that he never produced one without some excellent comic trait.'

There are snatches of Goldoni's plays with something of the satire of Molière, something of the farce of Feydeau, and they have a modern sophistication, with their levity at times on the brink of cynicism. They show us not so much how Goldini saw the Venetians as how the Venetians liked to see themselves. The same is true of the work of Pietro Longhi, whose series of genre paintings comment directly and charmingly on the domestic and public life of the different Venetian classes, marked during the Carnival or in the gambling rooms, playing music, going to the country, at their food, or staring thoughtfully at a rhinoceros brought to the City in 1751.

Goldoni's Venetians laughed at their own vices and follies quite gently and were pleased with being Venetians. In *The Artful Widow*, Rosaura tells her disappointed French suitor that she was glad to live in a country where commonsense was valued more than anywhere else. Her Italy taught the world how to live and selected the best from other nations. A natural question on the lips of the Venetians in Goldoni's comedies is how visitors like the city, and the answer is expected to be enthusiastic. Tonino, the intelligent brother of *The Venetian Twins*, declares that in Venice friendship is valued more than life itself and that all Venetians are the soul of honour.

In plays like spun-sugar, Goldoni held before the Venetians a mirror showing the smoothed, rouged, surfaces of Casanova's pock-marked Venice. The reassuringly traditional figures of Arlecchino and Pantalone move among flirtatious maidservants, lovely shrewd Venetian ladies, ardent Italian lovers and ridiculous lechers from abroad in a world of ever-lifting skirts and whirring fans. The pleasure-hunting, money-grabbing, marvellously articulate Venetians as they saw each other on stage.

'Truth,' Goldoni wrote in his charmingly reflective *Memoirs*, 'has always been my favourite virtue, and I have always been satisfied by her.'

The truth about eighteenth-century Venetians is especially elusive. The creative pulse beat strongly throughout the century in most parts of life except the political. Journalism was a brash, entertaining feature of Venice's liveliness, grafting English political approaches on to native Italian wit in the satirical weekly, *La*

Gazzetta Veneta, one of many literary gazettes written in Venetian and stuffed with good writing as well as gossip. In the fifteen-year reign of Doge Alvise IV Mocenigo starting in 1763, the Venetian navy acted bravely and vigorously to protect Venice's revived trade with the Levant against piracy. Just a few years before the fall of the Republic, the immense sea-walls of Istrian stone, defending the civilisation of the lagoon against high seas – the Murazzi – were completed in a great feat of civil engineering on the *lidi* to the south. Ironically, the last great poet given to Europe by the Venetian empire – Ugo Foscolo – was to welcome Napoleon with an ode of thanks for 'liberation'. Antonio Canova, who left for Rome in 1781, reflected glory on Venice whose patricians gave him his first important commissions, as the greatest of international neo-classic sculptors.

Do the generous Canova and the lyrical Foscolo speak for the truth of eighteenth-century Venice less than Casanova or Gozzi?

What was thought to be characteristic of Italy and Venice, for the English of the first half of the eighteenth century, was very much influenced by the austere opinions of the parson's son Joseph Addison who published his reflections at the age of thirty-three in 1705, under the title *Remarks on Several Parts of Italy, in the years 1701, 1702, 1703*. A moralist and an arbiter of conduct, this model English stylist of lightly exact prose, conscious of the enviable benefits to England of the Great Revolution, looked very coolly at the Italians, their institutions and their cities and his enthusiasm, when he does express it, gains all the more from his restraint.

'There is certainly no Place in the World where a Man may travel with greater Pleasure and Advantage than in Italy,' he wrote in the Preface. 'One finds something more Particular in the Face of the Country, and more astonishing in the Works of Nature, than can be met with in any other Part of Europe . . .'

From an England resting between wars, mindful of recent invasion, Addison's first concern was to establish the reasons for Venice's vaunted defensive strength. The 'most impregnable Town in *Europe*,' he discovered, stood four miles from the *terra firma*, had its sea entrance well guarded, boasted a well stocked Arsenal, and could even hold off famine through the fish that could be taken up in the very streets.

Addison's sense of Venice's political hardening of the arteries

Carnival festivities

was acute. The city's trade was far from flourishing, its manufactures of cloth, glass and silk excelled by those of other countries, partly because the nobles shunned trade. 'They are tenacious of old Laws and Customs to their great Prejudice, whereas a Trading Nation must be still for new Changes and Expedients, as different Junctures and Emergencies arise.'

But Venice delighted Addison's eyes, as it rose from the sea like a 'great Town half floated by a Deluge' and he discovered gondolas as magnificent as coaches with six horses, handsome bridges and noble Palaces. Pictures were the richest furnishings of the palaces, he remarked. 'The Rooms are generally hung with Gilt Leather which they cover on extraordinary Occasions with Tapestry, and Hangings of greater Value. The Flooring is a kind of Red Plaister made of Brick ground to Powder, and afterwards work'd into Mortar. It is rubbed with Oil, and makes a smooth, shining, and beautiful Surface.'

Already, Addison sounds the themes that were to dominate the reactions of a succession of visitors during the eighteenth century.

'The Carnival of *Venice* is every where talk'd of. The great Diversion of the Place at that time, as well as on all other high Occasions, is Masking. The *Venetians*, who are naturally Grave, love to give into the Follies and Entertainments of such Seasons, when dignified in a false Personage. They are indeed under a necessity of finding out Diversions that may agree with the Nature of the Place, and make some Amends for the Loss of several Pleasures, which may be met with on the Continent. These Dignities give Occasion to abundance of Love-Adventures; for there is something more intriguing in the Amours of *Venice*, than in those of other Countries, and I question not but the Secret History of a Carnival would make a Collection of very diverting Novels. Operas are another great Entertainment of this Season. The Poetry of them is generally as exquisitely ill as the Musick is good . . .

'The Comedies that I saw at *Venice*, or indeed in any other Part of *Italy*, are very indifferent, and more lewd than those of other Countries. Their Poets have no Notion of gentile Comedy, and fall into the most filthy double Meanings imaginable, when they have a mind to make their Audience merry.'

And how the Venetians loved spectacle, from time immemorial.

'On Holy-*Thursday*, among the several Shows that are yearly exhibited, I saw one that is odd enough, and particular to the *Venetians*. There is a Set of Artisans, who by the help of several Poles, which they lay a cross with each others Shoulders, build themselves up into a kind of Pyramid; so that you see a Pile of Men in the Air of four or five Rows rising one above another. The weight is so equally distributed, that every Man is very well able to bear his Part of it, the Stories, if I may so call them, growing less and less as they advance higher and higher. A little Boy represents the Point of the Pyramid, who, after a short Space, leaps off, with a great deal of Dexterity, into the Arms of one that catches him at the Bottom. In the same manner the whole Building falls to pieces.'

As Venice might fall, thought Addison, through its mighty error of conquering a land empire and neglecting the increase of its strength by sea, through which 'they might perhaps have had all the Islands of the *Archipelago* in their Hands, and, by Consequence, the greatest Fleet, and the most Seamen of any other State in *Europe*.'

Venetian cunning might keep the Republic secure, Addison added, for the Senate was one of the wisest councils in the world, though hardly honourable in the maxims by which it lived.

'The Preservation of the Republick is that to which all other Considerations submit. To encourage Idleness and Luxury in the Nobility; to cherish Ignorance and Licentiousness in the Clergy, to keep alive a continual Faction in the Common People, to connive at the Viciousness and Debauchery of Convents, to breed Dissentions among the Nobles of the *Terra Firma*, to treat a brave man with Scorn and Infamy: in short, to stick at nothing for the Publick Interest, are represented as the refined Parts of the *Venetian* wisdom.'

Addison damned Venice with faint praise. His limpidly tetchy remarks at the very start of the last century of Venetian independence etched in English imaginations the lines of a city of Popish vice. From a friend of his, however, at mid-century, emerges an altogether sunnier and more balanced impression of life in the City and on the mainland domain.

The pen writing is one of the liveliest, most engaging, and refreshingly direct to be found in English letters. A woman of early beauty, of headstrong character, passionate feelings and opinions, and of scandalous reputation, Lady Mary Wortley Montagu cast a judicious and experienced eye on the Venetians and reported most favourably on what she saw.

Her marriage – to Edward Wortley Montagu – began with elopement, and, after she had accompanied him on his diplomatic missions to the East (which inspired many of her brightest letters), ended in permanent separation. She lived on the Continent from 1739 till near her death in 1762. Her American biographer, Robert Halsband, has edited the only complete edition of the nine hundred or so letters of this *grande dame* of the eighteenth century, so erudite, intelligent, amusing and aristocratic. The daughter of a duke, and the correspondent in three languages of poets, philosophers and patricians among a multitude of friends and acquaintances, she was the perfect gossip.

Lady Mary was in Venice for about a year from 1739 to 1740. After staying a few years in Avignon and then in Brescia for ten years, she lived in Padua and Venice between 1756 and 1761.

Lady Mary Wortley Montagu

With a house in each city, according to Halsband, she made Venice her London and Padua her Twickenham.

Her husband had been with Addison during part of the latter's Grand Tour and there was no need to describe the Arsenal to him, she wrote in one of her letters to Wortley. But scattered through the correspondence from the Veneto are scores of evocative references to Venetian dress and manners, to the theatre, to footwarmers at the Opera and the distant mountains covered with snow.

She wrote, in November 1739, to Lady Pomfret, comparing Venice with London. She had arrived in Venice a few weeks previously travelling by *chaise* to Padua and then by *burchiello*. It was cold, but there was a bright clear sun. There were foreign ministers in Venice from all over the world; and she was being courted as if she were the only lady in the world.

'As to all the conveniences of life, they are to be had at very easy rates; and for those that love publick places, here are two play-houses and two operas constantly performed every night, at exceeding low prices . . . It is the fashion for the greatest ladies to walk the streets, which are admirably paved; and a mask, price sixpence, with a little cloak, and the head of a domino, the genteel dress to carry you everywhere. The greatest equipage is a gon-dola, that holds eight persons, and is the price of an English chair. And it is so much the established fashion for every body to live their own way, that nothing is more ridiculous than censuring the actions of another. This would be terrible in London, where we have little other diversion; but for me, who never found any pleasure in malice, I bless my destiny that has conducted me to a part where people are better employed than in talking of the affairs of their acquaintance . . .'

Writing to Lady Bute, in February 1760, she extols Venice at the slight expense of Paris, for its secluded refinement. The Carnival was over.

'Diversions have taken a more private, perhaps a more agreable, Turn. 'Tis the Fashion here to have little houses of retreat where

Gondola race

the Lady retires every evening at 7 or 8 o' the Clock, and is visited (by) all her Intimates of both Sexes, which commonly amount to 70 or 80 persons, where they have play, concerts of Music, sometimes dancing and always a handsome Collation . . . Whoever is well acquainted with Venice must own that it is the center of Pleasure, not so noisy, and in my opinion more refin'd than Paris.'

Her impressions formed on her first visit had been proven right: 'this Town is likely to be most agreable and the quietest place I can fix in,' she had written to her husband, when asking him to arrange for her books, papers and boxes to be shipped directly to Venice from the Thames, on the ship *Tygress* which had thirty guns and so was unlikely to be attacked by privateers. The Venetians, she discovered, adored the English. Shortly after she took a house in Padua, in 1756, because Venice seemed too expensive, she wrote to Lady Bute that snuff boxes were as much in fashion in Venice as in London. 'In General, all the Shops are full of English Merchandise, and they boast everything coming from London, in the same Style they us'd to do from Paris . . .'

The English in Venice, on the other hand, sometimes appalled her. She complained to Lady Pomfret (in June 1740) that the town was 'infested' with English 'who torment me as much as the frogs and lice did the palace of Pharoah, and are surprized that I will not suffer them to skip about my house from morning till night . . .' They were English of the lesser sort, sighed this highly class-conscious lady: 'I wish I knew a corner of the world inaccessible to petits-maitres and fine ladies.'

For her husband's sake, Lady Mary Wortley Montagu painstakingly described the Regatta of 4 May 1740. It seems not all that dissimilar from the revived regatta that is now joined in Venice with the ceremony of the wedding of the sea.

'It is a race of Boats; they are accompany'd by vessells which they call Piotes and Bichones, that are built at the Expence of the nobles and strangers that have a mind to display their magnificence. They are a sort of Machines, adorn'd with all that sculpture and gilding can do to make a shineing appcarance. Several of them cost £1,000 sterling and I believe none less than 500. They are row'd by Gondoliers dress'd in rich Habits suitable to what they represent. There was enough to them to look like a little Fleet, and I own I never saw a finer sight. It would be too long to describe every one in particular; I shall only name the principal. The Signora Pisani Mocenigo's represented the chariot of the night, drawn by 4 sea Horses, and showing the rising of the moon accompany'd with stars, the statues on each side representing the hours to the number of 24, row'd by Gondoliers in rich Liveries, which were chang'd 3 times, all of equal richness; and the decorations chang'd also to the dawn of Aurora and the midday Sun, the statues being new dress'd every time, the first in green, the 2nd time red, and the last blue, all equally lac'd with silver, there being 3 Races. Signor Soranzo represented the Kingdom of Poland with all the provinces and Rivers in that Dominions, with a consort of the best instrumental music in rich Polish Habits; the painting and gilding were exquisite in their kinds. Signor (Simoni) Contarini's Piote shew'd the Liberal Arts; Apollo was seated on the stern upon Mount Parnasso, Pegasus behind, and the muses seated round him. Opposite was a figure representing painting, with Fame blowing her Trumpet, and on each side Sculpture and music in their proper dresses. The Procurator Foscarini's was the chariot of Flora, guided by Cupids and adorn'd with all sorts of Flowers, rose trees, etc.

'Signor Julio Contarini represented the Triumphs of Valour; Victory was on the Stern, and all the Ornaments warlike Trophys of every kind. Signor Correri's was the Adriatic Sea receiving into her Arms the Hope of Saxony. Signor Alvisio Mocenigo's was the Garden of Hesperides. The whole Fable was represented by different Statues. Signor Querini had the chariot of Venus drawn by Doves, so well done they seem'd realy to fly upon the water; the Loves and Graces attended her.

'Signor Paul Dona had the chariot of Diana, who appear'd Hunting in a large wood, the trees, hounds, Stag and Nymphs all done naturally, the Gondoliers dress'd like peasants attending the chase, and Endimion lying under a large Tree gazing on the Goddess.

'Signor Angelo Labbia represented Poland crowning of Saxony, waited on by the Virtues and subject provinces. Signor Angelo Molino was Neptune waited on by the Rivers. Signor Vicenzo Morosini's Piote shew'd the Triumphs of Peace, discord being chain'd at her Feet, and she surrounded with the Pleasures, etc.

Dogana and Santa Maria della Salute by Guardi

'I believe you are allready weary of this description, which can give you but a very imperfect Idea of the show, but I must say one word of the Bichones, which are less vessels, quite open, some representing Gardens, others apartments, all the oars being gilt either with Gold or Silver, and the Gondoliers' Liverys either velvet or rich silk with a profusion of Lace fringe and Embrodiery. I saw this show at the Procurator Grimani's house, which was near the place where the Prizes were deliver'd. There was a great assembly invited on the same Occasion, which were all nobly entertain'd.

'I can get no better Ink here, tho I have try'd several times, and it is a great vexation to me to want it.'

Some of Lady Mary's ink was expended on praise not only of the pleasures but also of the politics of Venice. Sitting by the fireside, she wrote to Lady Pomfret in May 1740 that her 'strong notion' was that 'Venice is more agreeable than Florence, as freedom is more eligible than slavery . . .' She notes how shrewdly the rulers of Venice exploit the gambling instincts of their people by carefully regulating the Ridotto, writing to Wortley in 1750: 'I wonder you do not imitate at London the wise conduct of this State, who, when they found the rage of play untameable, invented a method to turn it to the Advantage of the Publick now Fools lose their Estates, and the Government profits by it.' In a letter to Lady Bute written in the summer of 1753, she gives a vivid picture of her political prejudices which solace in Venice for what was happening in England. She is reflecting on the death of her half-sister, Lady Caroline Brand, who had married beneath her (to a member of parliament). She had dishonoured her family by this 'mean marriage'.

'It may be you will call this an old fashion'd way of thinking. The confounding of all Ranks and making a Jest of order has long been growing in England, and I perceive, by the Books you sent me, has made a very considerable progress. The Heros and Heroines of the age are Coblers and Kitchin Wenches. Perhaps you will say I should not take my Ideas of the manners of the times from such trifling Authors, but it is more truly to be found amongst them than from any Historian. As they write meerly to get money, they allwaies fall into the notions that are most acceptable to the present Taste. It has long been the endeavour of our English writers to represent people of Quality as the vilest and silliest part of the Nation. Being (gennerally) very low born themselves, I am not surpriz'd at their propagateing this Doctrine, but I am much mistaken if this Levelling Principle does not one day or other break out in fatal consequences to the public, as it has allready done in many private Families.

'You will think I am influenc'd by living under an Aristocratic Government, where Distinction of Rank is carry'd to a very great height; But I can assure you my Opinion is founded on Refflection and Experience . . .'

It was precisely the 'Levelling Principle', historians have since reflected – the numbers of sisters and daughters who married beneath their class – that saved England from revolution; and it was the 'Distinction of Rank' among Venetians that drained off their allegiance to the dominant aristocracy and the Republic's demise. Even among the nobles (numbering a few hundred families out of a city population of about 140,000) gradations of rank were punctiliously observed.

Within the normally closed caste of the nobility, families were ranked in prestige and political importance according to the time in history when their ancestors were raised to the patriciate. A few great families traced their privileges back to the election of the first Doge; at the other extreme, the 'new families' had been ennobled in recent centuries, and included those who had paid for the honour. Wealth was essential to the pursuit of office; contrasting with the rich ducal councillors and state ambassadors – elected from the thousand or so noble members of the Great Council – were the Barnabotti, called so after the district where they mostly lived, poor, ill-educated and generally rather wretched though proud.

The economy of Venice, open to immigrant talent, adapted itself quite successfully to the new pressures of industrialisation and international trade during the eighteenth century. The political system, as Lady Mary rightly discerned, was essentially hostile to the spirit of democracy.

Jean-Jacques Rousseau, who like Voltaire was one of her correspondents, went to Venice for a year's cantankerous sojourn at the French embassy in 1743. There he conceived the idea of writing his *Institutions Politiques,* of which the *Contrat Social* is a part, and he carefully noted the nuances of aristocratic politics. Venice had an hereditary aristocracy, he wrote, which was the worst form of all; though, he reflected, Government at Venice was not a true aristocracy since all the poor nobles, the *Barnabotes,* never held office. The illustrious members of the Grand Council had no more privileges than the simple citizens of Geneva. 'As for the Council of Ten at Venice, it is a tribunal of blood, equally horrible to the patricians and to the people, and which, far from protecting the laws from on high, serves only, after they have been debased, to deal in the shadows blows that no one dare contemplate.'

In the Age of Enlightenment, the visitor to Venice ceased to look for the secrets of political success; the scholars, like the poets and the tourists, came for pleasure and art. Rousseau in his *Confessions* extolled the old-fashioned music of the *scuole,* and recalled being filled with an amorous trembling when he met the girls whose angel voices he had heard through the church grill. Music was so cheap in Italy, he exclaimed; and Venice was not the kind of town where a man abstained from women. Gibbon, who had once thought of writing the life of Sir Philip Sidney as his great historical essay, before his visit to Rome in October 1764 when he first thought he might write about its decline and fall, discovered that 'The spectacle of Venice afforded some hours of astonishment'. Voltaire, to reflect many of his own tastes and to express the heights of a pleasurable civilised life, constructed the personage of Count Pococurante, a noble Venetian, as host in his palace on the Brenta to Candide. Count Pococurante has two pretty girls to serve his cups of chocolate and warm his bed; a gallery with pictures by Raphael; his own musicians; a large and excellent library; and a beautiful garden. In Voltaire's Venice, the gondoliers are still singing; and a young monk with rosy cheeks always strolling arm in arm with his girl friend across St Mark's Square, and Count Pococurante for ever yawning over all the sensual and intellectual delights that are his in abundance.

As the carnivals come and go, the visitors to Venice increasingly carry in their emotional and intellectual luggage the fresh tones of romanticism. Venice present begins to merge into Venice past as an idealised, timeless expression of the fusion of man–made and natural beauty. Rousseau had no eye for painting or architecture; neither, save at exceptional moments, did Voltaire. Johann Wolfgang Goethe annexed Italy, as did Proust after him, to the whole of his past emotional life: *Alle Träume meiner Jugend seh ich nun lebendig* – 'I now realise all the dreams of my youth,' he wrote ecstatically when he reached Rome in the winter of 1786. His passion for history and his quest for beauty of face and form were allied to powerful scientific curiosity and genius of literary expression to render the Venice he first scrutinised in the autumn of that year with the realistic radiance of a supreme painter. The pages on Venice in his *Italian Journey* are rich in psychological perception and in images that float free of Goethe's own time.

'It was written, then, on my page in the Book of Fate that at five in the afternoon of the twenty-eight day of September in the year 1786, I should see Venice for the first time as I entered this beautiful island-city, this beaver-republic . . .' This is the appropriately solemn note, bringing German intensity to all the paradoxes of Venice, which Goethe sounds when introducing his reports from the Serenissima. He came down the Brenta from

Grand Canal and Palazzo Bembo

Padua, by the public boat, past wonderful gardens and palaces.

'At last we entered the lagoons and, immediately, gondolas swarmed round our boat. A passenger from Lombardy, a man well known in Venice, invited me to join him in one so that we might arrive in the city more quickly and avoid the ordeal of the Dogana. Some people wanted to detain us, but, with the help of a modest tip, we succeeded in shaking them off and, in the peaceful sunset, went gliding quickly towards our goal.'

Always searching for the causes of things, Goethe remarked on the 'sheer mass and instinctive existence' of the Venetian people, whose civilisation was driven forward by necessity from its very beginning. All the wonders he saw as he roamed the city were a stupendous monument 'not to one ruler, but to a whole people'. He sees the sea beyond for the first time from the top of the Campanile of San Marco; galleys and frigates at anchor in the lagoon are waiting for the winds to change before they leave to join the campaign against the Algerians. North and West, the hills of Padua and Vicenza and the Tyrolean Alps make a beautiful frame to the whole picture; but the next day, he is struck by the dirtiness of the streets.

With a few, confident verbal strokes, Goethe paints the scenes of Venice like Guardi. A group listens to a man on the quayside telling stories in the Venetian dialect: 'No one laughed, there was rarely even a smile. There was nothing obtrusive or ridiculous about his manner, which was even rather sober; at the same time the variety and precision of his gestures showed both art and intelligence.' He visits the opera in San Moisè and then the ballet, which was booed most of the time. 'But one or two of the dancers, male and female, were wildly applauded. The girls considered it their duty to acquaint the audience with every beautiful part of their bodies.' He witnessed with grave inquisitiveness a trial in the Palazzo Ducale. A scraggy clerk in a black coat starts reading, and 'only then did I realise the significance of a little man sitting on a low stool behind a little table, not far from the advocates' platform, and of the hourglass he had in front of him. So long as the clerk is reading, the time is not counted, but if the advocate wishes to interrupt the reading, he is granted only a limited time. When the clerk reads, the hourglass lies on its side with the little man's hand touching it. As soon as the advocate opens his mouth, the hourglass is raised; as soon as he stops talking, it is laid down again.' The opportunities for clowning are immense.

At night, under Goethe's bedroom at the Queen of England near San Marco, bedlam breaks loose after midnight. 'Whether for good or ill, they are always up to something together. Now I have heard three fellows telling stories on a square and a quay, also two lawyers, two preachers and a troupe of comic actors.'

At the Arsenal, Goethe is fascinated to study men working with Istrian oak; the new *Bucentaur* – a family heirloom for Venice – reminds him of what the Venetians once thought themselves to be, and were; the audience's behaviour at the theatre helps him to understand better the long speeches and passages of dialect in Greek tragedy.

The few pages of Goethe's descriptions of Venice – quoted here from the Penguin Classics translation by W. H. Auden and Elizabeth Mayer – are dense with allusion, every observation prompts a reflection and, in numerous slight ways, Venice plays its perennial role as a creative influence and intellectual stimulus. The *Italian Journey* is the best starting point for exploration of the mind and work of Goethe; Goethe's response to Italy is a critically important element in the evolution of attitudes to Venice, as to Rome. It is a little awesome to be reminded, as I once was by Professor Rolf Dahrendorf, of Goethe's 'over-towering presence'. There is everything, he said, in Goethe: 'It is deep and profound and universal . . .' But Goethe can be enjoyed, like Homer and Dante, at several levels. We can simply stare eagerly at Venice through his eyes, seeing it alive and direct and like a young, not a dying, city in the eighteenth century. For after all, 'the Venetians have little to worry about: the slowness with which the sea is receding guarantees them security for millennia, and, by intelligently improving their system of dredged channels, they will do their best to keep their possessions intact.'

Meanwhile, Goethe praises the dignity of Venice, as he saw it expressed on 7 October 1786, when he was thirty-seven.

'This morning I attended High Mass at the Church of Santa Giustina, where, on this day of the year, the Doge has always to be present to commemorate an old victory over the Turks. The gilded barges, carrying the Prince and some of the nobility, land at the little square; oddly-liveried boatmen ply their red-painted oars; on shore the clergy and religious orders, holding lighted candles on poles and silver candelabra, jostle each other and stand around waiting; gangways covered with carpets are laid across from the vessels to the shore; first come the Savii in their long violet robes, then the Senators in their red ones, and, last, the old Doge, in his long golden gown and ermine cape and wearing his golden Phrygian cap, leaves the barge while three servants bear the train of his robe.

'To watch all this happening in a little square before the doors of a church on which Turkish standards were displayed was like seeing an old tapestry of beautiful colour and design, and to me, as a fugitive from the north, it gave keen pleasure. At home, where short coats are *de rigueur* for all festive occasions and the finest ceremony we can imagine is a parade of shouldered muskets, an affair like this might look out of place, but here these trailing robes and unmilitary ceremonies are perfectly in keeping.

'The Doge is a good-looking, imposing man. Although, apparently, in ill health, he holds himself, for the sake of dignity, erect under his heavy gown. He looks like the grandpapa of the whole race and his manner is gracious and courteous. His

Goethe

garments were very becoming and the little transparent bonnet he wore under his cap did not offend the eye, for it rested upon the most lovely snow-white hair.

'He was accompanied by about fifty noblemen, most of them very good-looking. I did not see a single ugly one. Some were tall and had big heads, framed in blond curly wigs. As for their faces, the features were prominent and the flesh, though soft and white, had nothing repellently flabby about it. They looked rather intelligent, self-assured, unaffected and cheerful.

'When they had all taken their places in the church and High Mass had begun, the religious orders entered in pairs by the west door, were blessed with holy water, bowed to the high altar, to the Doge and to the nobility, and then left by a side door to the right.'

Goethe brooded on the 'sheer mass' of the Venetians and brought some few ordinary people anonymously to life. Mrs Thrale, the erstwhile friend of Samuel Johnson and Fanny Burney, published her *Observations and Reflections made in the course of a journey through France, Italy and Germany* in two volumes in 1789, the year of the French Revolution, and the year when Ludovico Manin became the last Doge of Venice. The widow of a rich Southwark brewer and M.P., the mother of eleven children, soundly educated and warm hearted, she married an Italian musician, Gabriele Piozzi, in 1780 and, estranged from the mortified Dr Johnson, travelled with her husband in Italy. She has a curious eye for the domestic parts of Venice, observing people closely in their individualities, presenting a city part holiday resort, part fairy-land, and apt to compare what she saw there with what went on at home in St James's Park or Richmond.

Refreshingly, after the loftiness of Goethe's inquisitive reaches, Mrs Thrale's prosaic, womanly eye brings to the fore an important and enduring aspect of Venice: the strange and unique environment, sea-girt and laced, of the everyday life of a people who see nothing extraordinary in the way they exist and view intruders and intrusions from outside as the real oddities.

'One has heard,' she recalls, 'of a horse being exhibited for a show there, and yesterday I watched the poor people paying a penny-a-piece for the sight of a stuffed one, and am more than persuaded of the truth of what I am told here – that numberless inhabitants live and die in this great capital, nor ever find out or think of inquiring how the milk brought from *terra firma* is originally produced.'

Very practically, like the idiosyncratic Burgundian Charles de Brosses who was in Venice in 1739 and complained that you could not take a step without putting your feet into water, she observed that the town could not be a wholesome one, 'for there is scarcely a possibility of taking exercise . . .' And it was disconcerting to say the least when she went to see Paul Veronese's painting of the marriage at Cana in Galilee, in St George's Church, to find that the picture was kept in a refectory to which no women were admitted.

'At my return to Venice I met little comfort, as everybody told me it was my own fault, for I might have put on men's clothes and see it whenever I pleased, as nobody then would stop, though perhaps all of them would know me.'

Like Goethe, she found the dirt and stink of parts of Venice a great shame: 'I do never cease to wonder that so little police and proper regulation are established in a city so particularly lovely to render her sweet and wholesome.' Like Rousseau, she observed that the ladies of Venice appeared to study but one science:

> And where the lesson taught
> Is but to please, can pleasure seem a fault?

Their sensuality, she comments, damages their looks and their health, and at thirty they have 'a wan and faded look'. However, Venetian woman are naturally sweet, with mellifluous voices and of diminutive stature. They wear little or no rouge, and increase their natural paleness by scarce light wiping of white powder from their faces. Their dress, when they appear out of doors in the morning, consists of the zendalet – a full black silk petticoat, training a little on the ground and flounced with gauze, and a large piece of black mode or persian thrown over a skeleton wire on the head, shading the face like a curtain, rolled back so as to discover the bosom, and fastened with a puff at the top of the stomacher.

'The evening ornament is a silk hat, shaped like a man's and of the same colour, with a white or worked lining at most, and sometimes one feather; a great black silk cloak, lined with white, and perhaps a narrow border down before, with a vast, heavy round handkerchief of black lace, which lies over neck and shoulders, and conceals shape and all completely. Here is surely little appearance of art, no craping or frizzing the hair, which is flat at the top and all of one length, hanging in long curls about the back or sides as it happens. No brown powder, and no rouge at all. Thus without variety does a Venetian lady contrive to delight the eye, and without much instruction, too, to charm the ear. A source of thought fairly cut off beside, in giving her no room to show taste in dress or invent new fancies and disposition of ornaments for tomorrow. The Government takes all that trouble off her hands, knows every pin she wears, and where to find her at any moment of the day or night.'

Mrs Thrale's political observations were equally homely and direct. Venice, she said, was a grain of monarchy, a scruple of democracy, a drachma of oligarchy, and an ounce of aristocracy – and 'the longevity of this incomparable commonwealth is certain proof of her temperance, exercise and cheerfullness, the great preservatives of every body, politic as well as natural'. Venice was a truly beloved ally of England; a lover of peace; a resister of change; a stronghold of patriotism, where all the ladies would part with their rings and bracelets to make ropes for the ships as they did in 1600, and a bulwark against the Turk – though vicinity to Turkey had encouraged some similarity of manners, such as the rage to drink great quantities of coffee. 'I have already had seven cups today, and feel frightened lest we should some of us be killed with so strange an abuse of it.'

On the other side of the Adriatic, Mrs Thrale revealed, they took opium to counteract the effects of coffee. 'But these dear Venetians have no notion of sleep being necessary to their existence, I believe, as some or other of them seem constantly in motion, and there is really no hour of the four-and-twenty in which the town seems perfectly still and quiet.'

The Veneto's beauty was marred for Mrs Thrale by the spectacle of so many paupers in the towns of the mainland 'tormenting passengers with unextinguishable clamour, and surrounding them with sights of horror unfit to be surveyed by any eyes except those of the surgeon . . .' But she showed a warm appreciation and left a brief moving description for us of the beauty of Venice at night, as it was and as it still almost is.

'Whoever sees St Mark's Place lighted up of an evening, adorned with every excellence of human art and pregnant with pleasure, expressed by intelligent countenances sparkling with every grace of nature, the sea washing its walls, the moonbeams dancing on its subjugated waves, sport and laughter resounding from the coffee-houses, girls with guitars skipping about the square, masks and merry-makers singing as they pass you, unless a barge

Piazza San Marco: Procuratie Vecchie and Ala Napoleonica

with a band of music is heard at some distance upon the water, and calls attention to sounds made sweeter by the element over which they are brought – whoever is led suddenly, I say, to this scene of seemingly perennial gaiety, will be apt to cry out of Venice, as Eve says to Adam in Milton:'

> *With thee conversing I forget all time,*
> *All seasons and their change – all please alike.'*

The collapse of the Venetian Republic in 1797 is customarily blamed on the decadence of its society, the conservatism of its government, and the pusillanimity of its rulers, especially Doge Manin from Friuli, one of the new men among the nobility, whom Napoleon frightened to tears and almost to death.

But Venice's stability and resilience during most of the eighteenth century against the background of shifting European frontiers and collapsing monarchies was remarkable. In *Candide*, in a dazzling passage of concentrated irony, Voltaire overhears Achmet III, dethroned Sultan, Ivan, former Emperor of all the Russians, Charles Edward, exiled King of England, two rejected Kings of Poland, the once-elected King of Corsica, and four defeated Serene Highnesses. They are all staying safely in Republican Venice, waiting for the Carnival.

An exceptional combination of political developments, like the combination of natural events that on rare occasions threatens to submerge Venice under the sea, lost Venice its old government and ancient freedom.

Austria – to whom the Venetians looked for support against Turkish power and French ambition – had long wanted to add

Horse of San Marco –
to France and back

Guardi selling his paintings outside Florian's

Venice to her empire. In 1778, the French ambassador in Vienna wrote that the Emperor's first objective to realise his ambitions in Italy would be the capture of Venice. The balance between France and Austria, which had safeguarded Venetian independence, suddenly tilted to the advantage of France in Italy through the astounding military successes of Napoleon. And Napoleon combined a growing hatred of Venice – for its aristocratic structures and for daring even to exist as a potential block to his will – with a shrewd assessment of its worth as a bargaining counter. Who can say how strong militarily and diplomatically Venice would have to have been, to out-manoeuvre and out-fight Napoleon?

You can buy prints in Venice of the scene in the Piazza San Marco on 13 December 1797 when the four bronze horses from the Palazzo Ducale, looted by Enrico Dandolo from Constantinople during the Fourth Crusade, were drawn by carts with six live horses apiece to the barges ready to ship them to Marseilles. Then you stroll to the Piazza and see them in place, though in recent years one has been missing either because it is undergoing treatment or (as in 1979) has been sent for exhibition in England

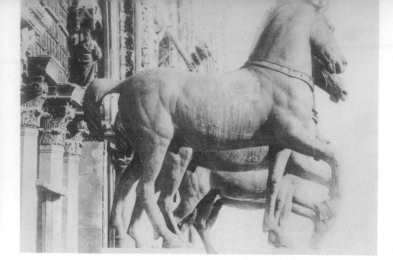

after the most delicate negotiations. Recently, too, there was a brisk argument over whether or not the horses should not be stabled indoors and replaced by replicas because of the ravages of weather. But historically, the laugh is on the French, who had to send the horses back from their places on the Arc du Carrousel, on 13 December 1815, at the demand of the Austrians.

Napoleon had raged against Venice when, as he drove against the Austrians in north Italy, violating Venetian territory, the people of Verona had risen against the French garrison (to be bloodily repressed) and the Venetian commander, Domenico Pizzamano, had bombarded a French schooner trying to force an entry at the Porto di Lido. (They were not the only examples of Venetian courage and loyalty to the old order.) He used ferocious threats and displays of anger to terrify the Venetian Doge and Senate into submission. The Grand Council was summoned on 12 May and, by 512 votes to twenty – an insufficient number according to the constitution – declared the Government at an end. Already Napoleon had negotiated preliminary peace terms with Austria which included the handing over of Venice to the Emperor. By the peace of Campoformio in October 1797 – a triumph for Napoleon as 'peacemaker' – Austria was to occupy Venice and gain possession of Istria, Friuli and Dalmatia. Belgium, in a breathtaking swap of territorial claims, went to France. Milan, Modena and Bologna were established as the Cisalpine Republic. During the months before Austrian troops moved into Venice in January 1798, French troops, French agents and collaborating Venetians throughout the Veneto and in Venice especially systematically listed, packed and despatched

Ducal Palace by Ruskin

to France immense quantities of weapons, documents, books, and art treasures of all kinds. The French army of Italy was given a flag by the Directory in Paris glorifying it for having 'made 150,000 prisoners, taken 170 flags, 540 artillery and siege guns, 5 bridges, 9 ships, 12 frigates, 12 corvettes, 18 galleys, given liberty to the people of the north of Italy, of Corcyre, of the Aegean Sea, of Ithica; sent to Paris the masterpieces of Michael Angelo, Guercino, Titian, Paolo Veronese, Correggio Albano, the Carraci, Raphael, etc.; triumphed in 18 pitched battles and fought 67 actions.'

The French poured back into Venice in 1805, after a series of resounding military victories over the Austrians, to rule for ten momentous years. In December 1804, Napoleon crowned himself Emperor in Notre Dame. The new Kingdom of Italy was proclaimed, and Venice was to be absorbed into it. On his brother's refusal, Napoleon took the kingship of Italy himself, and was consecrated on 26 May 1805, in the Cathedral of Milan, with the ancient iron crown of the Lombard kings. He visited Venice in 1807, amidst lavish ceremonies, and discussed great projects for its renewal and reconstruction of part of an empire that might also last hundreds of years.

But in 1815, under the Treaty of Paris, Venice was again ceded to Austria by the nations of the Holy Alliance, and another Emperor, now from Vienna, crossed the Alps to survey his domain.

Whereas the Austrians, during the occupation before 1805 and after 1815 tended to let the city softly rot, letting their soldiers grow vicious before signs of restlessness, the French, after the first spasm of looting, destroyed calmly and methodically in order to create in the image of the empire.

This meant the application of the Code Napoleon and a lurch towards the final secularisation of Venetian culture through the closures of religious houses and the confiscation of their wealth. The *scuole* were abolished for fear of their reactionary influence.

Under Napoleon's viceroy, Eugène de Beauharnais, but with the Emperor's direct involvement, whole sectors of Venice were torn down and rebuilt. The Academy Gallery, the Accademia, was founded by a decree issued by de Beauharnais in 1807, and benefited from the spoliation of the monasteries and guilds. The state granary overlooking the basin of San Marco was destroyed and gardens planted in its place. In the Piazza San Marco itself, the church of San Geminiano, which had been completed by Sansovino, 'like a ruby among many pearls' on the west, was demolished along with the continuations of the old *Procuratie Vecchie* and *Procuratie Nuove*, to build an *Ala Napoleonica*, with ballroom and staircase for the viceroy's apartments. The neo-classical building, which completes the trapezoid form of the Piazza in arcaded form, is not inspiring. You pass by or through it, today, on your way elsewhere, but it is part of the established image of the Piazza for thousands who have missed seeing pictures of the former church.

Napoleon, who threatened to be an Attila for Venice, destroyed its Republican independence and so part of its soul. Visitors, from England especially, tended to speak of Venice as the eighteenth century wore on in somewhat patronising terms; from now on – after humiliation by the French and the Austrians – it would tend to be in terms of pity. The teasing, unanswerable question, as one considers the importance in European history of Napoleon's personal ambition and energy, is what might have

Tiepolo's tumblers and clowns

been, had Venice survived those wars. And did the sordid destruction of Venetian independence make the maintenance of the city's cultural integrity and physical beauty impossible to sustain?

Venice found no allies when the Republic was assaulted and fell but the event has affected the imagination of many artists and writers with profound melancholy ever since. Wordsworth's sonnet stirs the heart with its old myths and images:

ON THE EXTINCTION OF THE VENETIAN REPUBLIC
(Composed probably August 1802 – Published 1807)

Once did She hold the gorgeous east in fee;
And was the safeguard of the west: the worth
Of Venice did not fall below her birth,
Venice, the eldest Child of Liberty.
She was a maiden City, bright and free;
No guile seduced, no force could violate;
And, when she took unto herself a Mate,
She must espouse the everlasting Sea.
And what if she had seen those glories fade,
Those titles vanish, and that strength decay;
Yet shall some tribute of regret be paid
When her long life hath reached its final day;
Men are we, and must grieve when even the Shade
Of that which once was great is passed away.

5 Paint and Paradox: the Dream City

In 1818, Byron's solicitor, John Hanson, arrived in Venice, bringing with him not the books which Byron had asked for, but an example of the kaleidoscope, recently perfected in its final form by Sir David Brewster. The 'damned S C O P E', as Byron called it, provides an image of Venice appropriate for the whole of the nineteenth century, when the most haunting, influential features of the city were found by visitors in its picturesqueness, its dazzling variety, its constant change from one startlingly graceful pattern to another. Venice proffered romanticism, the appealing combination of exotic history frozen in the timelessness of the past, and awesome Nature, undefiled by the satanic mills, always subtly, suddenly changing.

The beauty of Venice comes to seem too intense for words. Towards the end of the century, John Addington Symonds will write that 'Venice inspires at first an almost Corybantic rapture . . .' Horatio Brown will comment that even Turner, who came so near to grasping the spirit of the Venetian landscape, found that 'there were more tones in heaven and earth than dwelt upon his palate'. Frequently, the city floats free of time altogether in the observer's imagination and its vision is recalled as a dream. Byron in the Preface to his poem on the fourteenth-century conspiracy of the Doge Marino Faliero – 'one of the most remarkable events in the annals of the most singular government, city, and people of modern history' – writes that: 'Everything about Venice is, or was, extraordinary – her aspect is like a dream, and her history is like a romance.' Samuel Rogers, whose best-seller on *Italy*, a series of meditations in verse with beautiful steel engravings, appeared in 1830, recalls the approach to the 'glorious' Venice in this way:

> . . . *The path lies o'er the Sea,*
> *Invisible; and from the land we went,*
> *As to a floating City – steering in,*
> *And gliding up her streets as in a dream,*
> *So smoothly, silently – by many a dome,*

Mosque-like, and many a stately portico,
The statues ranged along an azure sky . . .

Charles Dickens, confounded by the alien Catholic civilisation of
Italy as much as by its antique beauty, recorded his impressions
of Venice in *Pictures of Italy* simply under the heading, 'An Italian
Dream'. Like Rogers, he has an alert eye for the horrific and the
macabre as well as the sheerly beautiful; as a novelist, he furnishes
and peoples the city.

'The glory of the day that broke upon me in this Dream; its
freshness, motion, buoyancy; its sparkles of the sun in water; its
clear blue sky and rustling air; no waking words can tell. But,
from my window, I looked down on boats and barks; on masts,
sails, cordage, flags; on groups of busy sailors, working at the
cargoes on these vessels; on wide quays, strewn with bales, casks,
merchandise of many kinds; islands, crowned with gorgeous
domes and turrets; and where golden crosses glittered in the
light, atop of wondrous churches, springing from the sea! Going
down upon the margin of the green sea, rolling on before the
door, and filling all the streets, I came upon a place of such
surpassing beauty, and such grandeur, that all the rest was poor
and faded, in comparison with its absorbing loveliness.

'It was a great Piazza, as I thought; anchored, like all the rest, in
the deep ocean . . .'

Dickens's 'dream' was more than a journalist's counterfeited emo-
tion; it was the literary coin appropriate to pay for an experience
stretching his sympathies beyond their reach. The dream
metaphor also, for English writers, helped to convey the unreal-
ity of contemporary Venice, conquered and corrupt, compared
with the full-blooded substance of the Venetian past.

In a scrap of dialogue in Disraeli's novel, *Contarini Fleming*, in a
Venice shimmering with gallantry and masked balls, the heroine
Alceste tells her cousin: 'I have no choice but to die where I was
born, and no wish to quit a country from which spring all my
associations; but you, you have a real country, full of real interests, to engage your affections and exercise your duties. In the
north, you are a man; your career may be active, intelligent and
useful; but the life of a Venetian is like a dream, and you must
pass your days like a ghost gliding about a city fading in a vision.'

Grand Canal by Turner

And in the novel *Venetia*, Disraeli, who heard tales of Byron's Venice from the gondolier Giovanni Battista Faliceri (Tita), reflects through the mind of Lady Annabel Herbert, as she approaches Venice, that, even before the fall of the Republic, the 'city without sound' with its fantastic architecture, glowing sky, flitting gondolas and brilliant crowd 'seemed a dream'.

Browning from his first visit to Asolo and Venice in 1838 fed some thin inspiration into *Pippa Passes* and *In A Gondola*; but the Venice which Elizabeth Barrett Browning found pitched between heaven and earth and on which Browning meditated profoundly later in life became for him above all a place in which to recall the pleasures of his own past. For his great poetry, Venice directly provided nothing substantial. Courtesy prompted his charming sonnet to Goldoni, when the statue was erected in 1883 in Campo San Bartolomeo. Asolo, not Venice, provided the title for the brilliant clutch of poems – *Asolando* – published the day he died in Venice; and amongst them *Ponte dell' Angelo Venice* is a medieval story. Browning's most direct evocations of Venice are

127

in letters from the Albergo dell'Universo about visiting the Countess Mocenigo and seeing the rooms in her palace which Byron had occupied ('I wrote my name in her album on the desk himself wrote the last canto of *Ch. Harold* and *Beppo* upon . . .'); and from the Ca' Alvisi, about the start of his autumn days:

'Every morning at six, I see the sun rise; far more wonderfully, to my mind, than his famous setting, which everybody glorifies. My bedroom window commands a perfect view: the still grey lagune, the few seagulls flying, the islet of S. Giorgio in deep shadow, and the clouds in a long purple rack, behind which a sort of spirit of rose burns up till presently all the rims are on fire with gold, and last of all the orb sends before it a long column of its own essence apparently: so my day begins.'

In English poetry, the romantics' dream of the Venetian landscape found its finest expression through the genius of Shelley, who sailed into the city in a black gondola, in 1818. Venice – like Byron, the fire that drew him there – alternately fascinated and repulsed Shelley. From the creative conflict he spun one of his great, strong compositions, the Venetian poem *Julian and Maddalo*, in which Julian is himself, Maddalo, Lord Byron. The Venetian setting, the lagoon, provides a beginning and end for the poem, and a counterpoint of descriptive brilliance for the whole, tense psychological drama. It paints Venice at a particularly important moment of literary history, and for all time.

First the encounter.

> *I rode one evening with Count Maddalo*
> *Upon the bank of land which breaks the flow*
> *Of Adria towards Venice: a bare strand*
> *Of hillocks, heaped from ever-shifting sand,*
> *Matted with thistles and amphibious weeds,*
> *Such as from earth's embrace the salt ooze breeds,*
> *Is this; an uninhabited seaside,*
> *Which the lone fisher, when his nets are dried,*
> *Abandons; and no other object breaks*
> *The waste, but one dwarf tree and some few stakes*
> *Broken and unrepaired, and the tide makes*
> *A narrow space of level sand thereon,*
> *Where 'twas our wont to ride while day went down.*

This ride was my delight. I love all waste
And solitary places; where we taste
The pleasure of believing what we see
Is boundless, as we wish our souls to be:
And such was this wide ocean, and this shore
More barren than its billows; and yet more
Than all, with a remembered friend I love
To ride as I then rode; — for the winds drove
The living spray along the sunny air
Into our faces; the blue heavens were bare,
Stripped to their depths by the awakening north;
And, from the waves, sound like delight broke forth
Harmonizing with solitude, and sent
Into our hearts aerial merriment . . .
As those who pause on some delightful way,
Though bent on pleasant pilgrimage, we stood,
Looking upon the evening and the flood,
Which lay between the city and the shore,
Paved with the image of the sky: the hoar
And aery Alps, towards the north, appeared,
Through mist, an heaven-sustaining bulwark, reared
Between the east and west; and half the sky
Was roofed with clouds of rich emblazonry,
Dark purple at the zenith, which still grew
Down the steep west into a wondrous hue
Brighter than burning gold, even to the rent
Where the swift sun yet paused in his descent
Among the many folded hills — they were
Those famous Euganean hills, which bear,
As seen from Lido, through the harbour piles,
The likeness of a clump of peaked isles —
And then, as if the earth and sea had been
Dissolved into one lake of fire, were seen
Those mountains towering, as from waves of flame,
Around the vaporous sun, from which there came
The inmost purple spirit of light, and made
Their very peaks transparent. 'Ere it fade,'
Said my companion, 'I will show you soon
A better station.' So, o'er the lagune
We glided; and from that funereal bark

I leaned, and saw the city, and could mark
How from their many isles, in evening's gleam,
Its temples and its palaces did seem
Like fabrics of enchantment piled to heaven,
I was about to speak, when – 'We are even
Now at the point I meant,' said Maddalo,
And bade the gondolieri cease to row.

And at the end.

If I had been an unconnected man,
I, from this moment, should have formed some plan
Never to leave sweet Venice: for to me
It was delight to ride by the lone sea;
And then the town is silent – one may write,
Or read in gondolas by day or night,
Having the little brazen lamp alight,
Unseen, uninterrupted: – books are there,
Pictures, and casts from all those statues fair
Which were twin-born with poetry; – and all
We seek in towns, with little to recall
Regret for the green country: – I might sit
In Maddalo's great palace, and his wit
And subtle talk would cheer the winter night,
And make me know myself: – and the firelight
Would flash upon our faces, till the day
Might dawn, and make me wonder at my stay.

English poets and painters added mixed distinction to the tens of thousands of tourists who journeyed to Italy after 1815, as the Grand Tour almost totally changed its character under the influences of easier travel and an increasingly monied middle-class. During the years of Austrian rule, Wordsworth was there and Coleridge; Rogers and Walter Savage Landor; Byron and Shelley, Thomas Moore and Keats and Clough. Pre-eminent among the painters was William Turner who first went to Italy in 1819, spending about a fortnight in Venice, which he visited again in 1835 and 1840. The water and the sky of Venice also attracted Bonington, who learned from Venetian painters, Edward Pritchett, who produced exquisite detailed little scenes and became known as the English *'genius loci'* of the city, and

Shelley

James Baker Pyne, from Bristol, whose restful works have come to be highly valued.

The revelation of the light of Venice to Turner is fixed in his sketches, watercolours and oils, in pale fused colours and 'tinted steam', from the first studies of 1819 to the silken atmospheric power of the large oils such as 'The Dogano, San Giorgio, Citella from the Steps of the Europa.' In all the pictures, there is a melancholy magic and a coldness in their very splash of colour and luminosity. In this respect, Turner's impressions of Venice betray the unease characteristic of most of the images created by visitors there during Austrian dominance. In the thoughtful Epilogue to his book on Venice, Peter Lauritzen writes that all the great nineteenth-century artists associated with Venice brought their own culture to it; that though he tried to live as a Venetian, Byron understood Venice merely through guide-books; and that Turner's Venetian paintings say a great deal that is interesting about Turner but 'remarkably little about Venice . . .'

But who knows what Turner learned and thought to express as he stared at the Venetian landscape? Certainly, the small Turner engraving I have by me now of its own brings the spirit of Venetian pride, elegance and strange commerce into my room, and the pale, moving light. Nonetheless, the subject of Venice did seem to inspire a certain evasion and distaste, at times a loathing, among the English poets and painters, who set their eyes on the water and the sky and the mountains, anywhere rather than on the city and its people.

Ruskin, drowning dissent with the force of those long sentences surging like waves that seem as if they will never break, reinforced lack of interest in living, contemporary Venice by loving the past only too passionately and too well. He studied in Venice over a period of seventeen years before publishing the fruits of his enraptured scrutiny in *Stones of Venice* in 1851. In this labyrinthine hymn to Venice's embalmed greatness, we occasionally hear the voices of live Venetians, the singing of children or gondoliers, but the organ of Ruskin's descriptive prose sounds most gorgeously and triumphantly for Venice preserved in stone from the time when the city practised true religion, *vital* individual religion and when, Ruskin reminded his English readers pointedly, the Venetians in admirable unity applied in their building principles which left the remains of the place as the 'richest existing examples of architecture raised by a mercantile community, for civil uses, and domestic magnificence.'

Ruskin bids us to hurry with him to the beautiful dead heart of Venice, quickly past the 'frightful façade of San Moisè, disdainfully past 'the mingling with the lower Venetian populace of lounging groups of English and Austrians'. He writes in tense ecstasy:

'We will push fast through them into the shadow of the pillars at the end of the "Bocca di Piazza", and then we forget them all; for between those pillars there opens a great light, and, in the midst of it, as we advance slowly, the vast tower of St Mark seems to lift itself visibly forth from the level field of chequered stones; and, on each side, the countless arches prolong themselves into ranged symmetry, as if the rugged and irregular houses that pressed together above us in the dark alley had been struck back into sudden obedience and lovely order, and all their rude casements and broken walls had been transformed into arches charged with goodly sculpture, and fluted shafts of delicate stone. And well may they fall back, for beyond those troops of ordered arches there rises a vision out of the earth, and all the great square seems to have opened from it in a kind of awe, that we may see it far away – a multitude of pillars and white domes, clustered into a long low pyramid of coloured light; a treasure-heap, it seems, partly of gold, and partly of opal and mother-of-pearl, hollowed beneath into five great vaulted porches, ceiled with fair mosaic, and beset with sculpture of alabaster, clear as amber and delicate as ivory – sculpture fantastic and involved, of palm leaves and lilies, and grapes and pomegranates, and birds clinging and fluttering among the branches, all twined together into an endless network of buds and plumes; and, in the midst of it, the solemn forms of angels, sceptred, and robed to the feet, and leaning to each other across the gates, their figures indistinct among the gleaming of the golden ground through the leaves beside them, interrupted and dim, like the morning light as it faded back among the branches of Eden, when first its gates were angel-guarded long ago. And round the walls of the porches there are set pillars of variegated stones, jasper and porphyry, and deep-green serpentine spotted with flakes of snow, and marbles, that half refuse and half yield to the sunshine, Cleopatra-like, "their bluest veins to kiss" – the shadow, as it steals back from them, revealing line after line of azure undulation, as a receding tide leaves the waved sand; their capitals rich with interwoven tracery, rooted knots of herbage, and drifting leaves of acanthus and vine, and mystical signs, all beginning and ending in the Cross; and above them, in the broad archivolts, a continuous

Piazza San Marco

chain of language and of life – angels, and the signs of heaven, and the labours of men, each in its appointed season upon the earth; and above these, another range of glittering pinnacles, mixed with white arches edged with scarlet flowers – a confusion of delight, amidst which the breasts of the Greek horses are seen blazing in their breadth of golden strength, and the St Mark's Lion, lifted on a blue field covered with stars, until at last, as if in ecstasy, the crests of the arches break into a marble foam, and toss themselves far into the blue sky in flashes and wreaths of sculptured spray, as if the breakers on the Lido shore had been frostbound before they fell, and the sea-nymphs had inlaid them with coral and amethyst.'

To find the Venetians, whom Ruskin briskly passes by, lisping their soft language, we have to turn from painters and poets to more prosaic and sympathetic letter writers and diarists such as William Stuart Rose and Lady Blessington d'Orsay. In letters to Henry Hallam, the great Whig historian, and the father of Tennyson's friend, William Rose described conditions in the North of Italy as the country settled down fitfully under the Austrian Imperial eagle to its years of revolution and reaction, called the age of Metternich.

Rose (whose two volumes of *Letters from the North of Italy* I discovered in Figgis' bookshop, Dublin, along with a first edition of Byron's *Marino Faliero*) was an old Etonian, who had studied at Christ Church, Oxford, and been an M.P. before applying for the Chiltern Hundreds to become a clerk of the House of Lords and spend his days travelling and writing. He translated Ariosto's *Orlando Furioso* at the urging of his friend Sir Walter Scott and with some help from the Italian patriot and poet, Ugo Foscolo, so taking an honourable place in a long line of brave translators of that delectable masterpiece, from Sir John Harington to Guido Waldman and Barbara Reynolds. He was rich, shrewd and cultured; an excellent and only occasionally pompous companion in Venice; as he tells us about the Venetian dialect and Venetian poetry and music; about the Austrian Government; about the Venetian character; the architecture of St Mark's and a fire in Ca' Corner.

Rose's eye is sharp and sympathetic. He finds that the Venetians, and the Florentines, are as droll as the Irish, and his

134

Ruskin

philosophical and political reflections spring from observant and lively reporting. He is quite knowing about food and drink and prices, as well as human nature.

In November 1817, Rose is *en route* from Padua to Venice, murmuring lines from Dante as he goes. He describes the villas and their garden ornaments and turnpike-roads between them and the Brenta, which stagnates into a canal traversing marshy meadows; he is curious about the way gondoliers handle their oars ('Your own *Canalettos* will have given you a better idea of the gondola than I could convey . . .') and relieved after his arrival and delay at Fusina, where luggage had to be landed and taxed, that the threatened *caligo* or mist does not prevent a swift passage across the lagoon and safe landing at Venice.

Society there, Rose quips, is like the fire in the glass-houses of London, it is never out. One lady or another is always 'at home' in the mornings, encouraging gatherings which appeared to substitute for the old gambling *casinos*. The *commedia dell'arte* flourishes, with *Pantaloon, Tartaglia*, (the stutterer), and *Doctor Balanzone, Harlequin* and *Brighella*. Goldoni's plays, Rose writes sniffingly, are in singularly poor taste; they display gross ignorance, not least when they scoff at Englishmen, but contain good strokes of humour when dealing with Venetian matters. They have driven the 'masques' off the stage, though Carlo Gozzi had secured these a brief and brilliant rally. The theatres are abundant in Venice as in every other Italian city, but the actors are haphazardly recruited and sloven. 'Let an Englishman, therefore, conceive a Hamlet soliloquising in broad Yorkshire, and he may guess at the feelings of a Florentine on hearing, as I have heard, the lyrical effusions of a David from Bergamo . . .' But the theatres are above all places of pleasant resort, cool and cheap. '. . . the post of honour in a box reserved for the lady is not that from which she can have the best view of the stage, but that from which she can be best seen by the audience . . .'

The replacement of the rule of the French by the rule of Austria (one of the 'sour crout' nations, remarks Rose ungraciously) may not have been entirely disadvantageous as far as the theatre is concerned. The French biographer of Haydn and Mozart, L. A. C. Bombet, who visited Venice in 1814, wrote telling a friend how disappointed he was to seek in vain for the plays of Gozzi and the commedia dell'arte and to find only translations from the French theatre: *Punch*, in the Piazza San Marco, afforded him more amusement.

After passing Christmas in Venice, Rose reflects thoughtfully on Venetian eating habits.

'For the Venetian holidays I have mentioned there are set dishes, as there are with us, and some of them of as strange composition: witness, one of fruits, preserved with sugar, spices, and mustard, which is the Venetian equivalent for a minced-pie. For the rest, the fare of Christmas eve, though meagre, is, as I have said, magnificent, always bating a sort of pye-pottage, called "torta de lasagne", which might, I suppose, pair off with plum-porridge itself.

'There is indeed one circumstance very favourable to the meagre department of the kitchen. The Mediterranean and Adriatic, in addition to most of those of our own coasts, have various delicate fish which are not to be found in the British seas.

Goldoni

Of the tunny, sword-fish, and many others of the larger classes, you have of course read. Some others, which are rare with us, as the red mullet, swarm in these latitudes; and some tribes which are known to us, here break into varieties which are infinitely better flavoured than the parent stock. Amongst such may be reckoned a sort of lobster, a crab of gentler kind, and various shell fish, entitled sea fruit in Italy, all which might well merit the eloquence of an Athenaeus.

'But not to pass by the "torta de lasagne", of which I had nearly lost sight, though its taste is fresh in my recollection: it is composed of oil, onions, paste, parsley, pine-nuts, raisins, currants, and candied orange peel, a dish which, you will recollect, is to serve as a prologue to fish or flesh!

'It ought, however, to be stated that the ordinary pottage of this country, and which is, generally speaking, that of all ranks in Venice, requires no prejudices of education or habit to make it go down, but may be considered as a dish to be eat at sight. It consists in rice boiled in beef broth, not sodden, and "rari nantes", as in England and France, but firm, and in such quantity as to nearly, or quite, absorb the "bouillon" in which they are cooked: To this is added grated Parmesan cheese. And the mess admits other additions, as tomatos, onions, celery, parsley, etc. Rice thus dressed, which have drunk up the broth, are termed "risi destirai", as capable of being spread, right or left, with the spoon. There is also a vulgar variety of the dish, termed "risi a la bechera", or rice dressed butcher fashion. In this the principal auxiliary is marrow, which, if it is entirely incorporated in the grain, makes a pottage that (speaking after a friend) would almost justify the sacrifice of an Esau.

'The mode of cooking the rice to a just degree of consistency, seems taken from the Turks, who have a saying that rice, as a proof of being well drest, should be capable of being counted. You will recollect the importance attached to this grain by the Janissaries, whose rice-kettles serve as standards; and, in general, by the Turkish militia, which is recruited by parading them, and calling for the services of such as eat the rice of the Grand Signior. An almost equal degree of respect is attached to this food by the Venetians, and it is a common thing, on hiring a Venetian maid-servant, for her to stipulate for a certain monthly salary, and her rice.

Banquet at the Polignac Wedding

'Another custom, derived from the long intercourse of Venice with Turkey, is the presenting coffee at visits. Neither do the Venetians yield to their masters in the manufacture of this beverage, the flavour of which depends much more on its mode of preparation than its quality; and it is curious enough that England, where the coffee-berry and the cacao-nut are to be had in perfection, should be the only country in Europe where the drink which is composed from them is unsufferable.'

Rose's letters lavish praise and blame open-handedly on the lovable people as well as the food of Venice. As he walks the streets, he is struck by a universal spirit of kindness.

'I never visited any country, where the people seemed equally linked in love . . . you hear continually *"caro pare"* and *"caro fio"* from the mouth of the lowest of the mob . . . The Venetians really give you the idea of being members of one great family . . . the Venetians were very distinguished for great originality of character, though this has been depressed under the iron crown of France and the leaden sceptre of Austria.'

Eccentrics abound, but with some ignoble traits.

'Take *one*: A Venetian, who died not very long ago, made a provision of torches for his funeral, artificially loaded with crackers, anticipating, to a confidential friend, the hubbub that would result from the explosion; which he had calculated must take place in the most inconvenient spots. It would be an unpardonable omission were I not to state that this posthumous joke verified the most sanguine expectations of its projector.'

The mercantile character of the Venetians, once so high, has deteriorated largely because of the Austrian legal and fiscal system. 'Alas, the whole fabric is rotten, the whole code, civil and criminal . . . By our English standard, I have never met with an honest banker in Italy.'

When he comes to discussing the nobles of Venice, Rose confesses that every detail of the picture is painful. The old poor nobility, the *Barnabotti*, dependent on the employments of the republic, were ruined by the revolution. When the law of *fedecommesso* (entail) was abolished, the encumbered property of the nobles – the *sangue blo*, the blue-blooded, and the *morel de mezo*, the ones in the middle   was immediately seized. For their daughters, place and pension disappeared. And today: 'The great political revolution that has taken place, destroying the splendour of the *libro d'oro*, has induced some to produce their *terra firma* titles; but the majority content themselves with the style of *Cavaliere* . . .'

Rose's pen splutters furiously as he castigates the Austrians for their greedy brutality in Italy. '*Sara fatto*', said the Austrian Emperor when he visited Venice in 1815, to the 40,000 petitions presented him, and no single promise had been fulfilled. The Venetian governor of the fortress of the Lido who had fired on and repulsed a French brig before the revolution in Venice, punished by Bonaparte, sought grace from the Emperor who promised assistance, but died neglected and in misery – 'and one of his sons is now employed in piecing the tesselated pavement in the church of St Mark!'

No wonder, Rose now sees clearly, that the Venetians preferred French rule to the government of the Austrians, 'a race which seems rather Chinese than European.' And in the last of his letters to Hallam, he warns: 'For the present, a recollection of their past sufferings and the necessity of repose, keeps the Italians quiet; but these are only temporary sedatives, and begin to wear out. The mine is charged anew, and if any accident gives it fire, half Europe will be shattered by the shock.'

Till 1848, however, Venice stayed comparatively passive, part of the Austrian Empire and yoked to Lombardy, under the Emperor Francis as king and an archduke as viceroy. Austrian troops in the north, always ready in support of other despotisms in Italy by their presence served at least to heighten the nationalist tension throughout the peninsular fostered by the French Revolution and the Napoleonic invasion. The Venetians kept their pride, and their gaiety; more and more, the visitors supplied the patina of romance. How beautiful the Piazza of San Marco still was, despite the shock of seeing the glorious standard of St Mark replaced by the spread eagle of Austria! 'I can well understand the feelings of the English child, who on beholding it for the first time, asked her mother if people were permitted to see it every day, or only on Sundays', exclaimed Lady Blessington d'Orsay, whose three-volume *The Idler in Italy* published in 1840 recalled the brief excitement of her sojourn there in 1828.

The Countess of Blessington swept the city's wonders calculatingly into the net of her recollections of years of continental wandering with a scandalous entourage. Her extraordinary life story has been deftly unravelled in a work of imaginative psychological detection, Michael Sadleir's *Blessington-d'Orsay: A Masquerade*.

The future Marguerite, Countess of Blessington was born in Tipperary in 1789 as Sally Power, the daughter of a vain, drunken and traitorous father who sold her in marriage to an English captain by whom she was brutally treated. Later she fled to Hampshire, England, with another English officer with whom she lived for several years developing sensational qualities of mind, beauty and charm, before being virtually sold as companion and subsequently wife to the Earl of Blessington, a rich, soft and amiable fool. Across their path in high society came the blithe figure of a young French dandy, Alfred, Comte d'Orsay et du Saint Empire, on whom Lord Blessington and Marguerite were soon, in their different fashions, both doting. Sadleir's theory is that the Countess and Alfred were respectively incapable of sexual response and impotent. The passionate triangle

Count d'Orsay

Earl of Blessington

Countess of
Blessington

was queerly innocent as was the subsequent Blessington-d'Orsay ménage but it scandalised London, and prompted a spreading sense of outrage sustained by Lady Blessington's variously gay and sordid exploits and experiences as widow, traveller, novelist, editor, fading beauty and financial wreck.

She was the friend of Rogers, Byron, Bulwer, Landor and Dickens, among other literary notabilities including Disraeli, who consulted her when revising his novel, *Venetia*, in 1837. She, and Blessington, with their pack of attendants, set out for an eccentric progress around France, Switzerland and Italy in 1822 on a whim, a fancy, created by the irresistible pleading of Alfred d'Orsay and his word that if they travelled the continent, he would be there as companion.

Because of these infatuations, we have from the pen of Marguerite Blessington-d'Orsay some moving recollections of Byron whom she met at Genoa (chiefly in her *Conversations of Lord*

Byron with the Countess of Blessington) and about a hundred printed pages on Venice, sentimental, evocative, wafting to us the sounds and smells of the city as experienced eagerly by a strange and meltingly beautiful, soundly self-educated, witty, intelligent and mature woman of forty in the atmosphere of the Regency, the Holy Alliance.

In Venice, staying at the Leone Bianco (comfortable, but by Austrian decree no French wine at dinner) Lady Blessington began her collection of objects that had once belonged to famous people with the purchase of an inkstand once owned by a Doge. She recalls she had bought some specimens of the old Venetian glass and some curious cameos. In the ante-room by her apartments, an Italian Jew pesters her daily in broken English to buy the inkstand of the last Doge, Manin. 'I ventured to insinuate that had it been the inkstand of Paolo Luca Anafesto, the first instead of the last Doge, it would have had more attractions for me.'

In the end, she became the owner of 'Manini's inkstand; the inkstand in which he dipped his pen to sign the capitulation of Venice after it had counted twelve centuries of sway.'

The lament for Venice's past glories is now becoming routine: Lady Blessington quotes Byron's magical lines beginning 'I stood at Venice on the Bridge of Sighs . . .' Each visitor now, like Byron ('Her palaces are crumbling to the shore') must remark on the sad evidences of physical decline. Lady Blessington's unhappiness on leaving Venice was increased 'by the knowledge that every year, nay, every month, takes away some charm from this fast decaying, but most picturesque of all cities.'

The nostalgia is not just imported by the visitor but more and more is becoming a large segment of Venetians' loyal image of their own city. 'I observe', Lady Blessington wrote, 'that the Venetian *cicerone* and gondoliers often refer to the past prosperity of Venice, and always in a tone that shows a knowledge of its history, and a pride of its ancient splendour not to be expected from persons of that class. There is something very touching in this sensibility . . .' She also stressed the bitterness of the Venetians towards their Austrian overlords. 'Even when ridiculing these unwelcome guests, the contemptuousness of the epithets they bestow on them have more of hatred than jocularity, though they aim at jesting.' She herself finds Austrians steady and restrained, though she must have wrinkled her nose on

Venice by Turner

her first arrival in the city when she saw that windows whose architraves were supported by exquisite caryatids were blocked up and showed the protruding iron pipes of German stoves, whose murky vapours profaned the sky, while over balustrades 'of marble, where once beauty loved to lean, float the unseemly nether garments suspended to be dried, of the Teutonic inhabitants who now fill those sculptured dwellings with the mingled odours of cigars and garlick; and mutter the guttural sounds of their language, where once the dulcet ones of the softest of all the Italian dialects, were wont to be heard.'

Other more sombre aspects of Venice made Lady Blessington shudder romantically as she linked the practice of secret denunciation with the retribution of defeat and decay. Everywhere are disturbing echoes of the past. The sight of the Bridge of Sighs reminds her – as she ponders the close proximity of pleasure and despair – of an incident from her first ball as a young girl in Ireland – a mother's shriek as her son was led away to be shot. In the Palazzo Mocenigo she is haunted by recollection of Byron, and obsessed by repellent imaginings of the orgies that had occurred where she stood. The Arsenal, now employing only

800 or 1,000 men with little to do, again reminds her of the fallen pride of Venice. A visit to a mad-house on one of the little islands in the lagoon inspires a harrowing description of Dickensian grotesqueness and pathos. When she is shown the house where Lady Mary Wortley Montagu lived she writes, perhaps self-revealingly, of the doubtless innocent nature of the relationship between her and her Algarotti, and the viciousness of scandal. The Four Horses, back in position over the western porch of St Mark's, she calls the steeds of victory – always the prize of the victor over the centuries – and she notes the curious coincidence that when yielded up to the Austrian government in 1815, the captain of the ship that re-conveyed them to Venice was a descendant of the Dandolo who originally won them for her.

Lady Blessington confessed herself an admirer of the Venetian school of painters. But they, too, are past glories, and a reproach to the present. The beauty she finds best to praise in Venice, and recalls most memorably, is the romantic beauty of nature and of the night.

'The silence of Venice constitutes, in my opinion, one of its greatest charms. This absence of noise is peculiarly soothing to the mind, and disposes it to contemplation. I looked out from my balcony last night, when the grand canal reflected a thousand brilliant stars on its water, turbid though it be; and the lights streaming from the windows on each side, showed like golden columns on its bosom. Gondola after gondola glided along, from some of which soft music stole on the ear, and sometimes their open windows revealed some youthful couple with their guitars, or some more matured ones, partaking their light repast of fruit and cakes; while not unfrequently a solitary male figure was seen reclined on the seat absorbed in the perusal of some book. The scene realised some of the descriptions of Venice read years ago; and except that the gondolas were small in number; and the lights from the houses few and far between, I could have fancied that no change had occurred since the descriptions I referred to were written. The morning light reveals the melancholy alteration; and as I stood on the same balcony to-day, and saw the muddy canal with a few straggling gondolas gliding over it, the defaced and mutilated palaces, and the reduced population, all brought out into distinctness by the bright beams of the sun, I could hardly believe it was the same scene that looked so well last night. Moonlight is a great beautifier, and especially of all that has been touched by the finger of decay, from a palace to – a woman. It softens what is harsh, renders fairer what is fair, and disposes the mind to a tender melancholy in harmony with all around.'

Unlike many of the romantic poets, Marguerite Blessington-d'Orsay, during her few weeks in Venice, did at least observe something of the people, though like the poets she was emotionally ambiguous in her reactions to the 'touch of decay'. Not a few distinguished visitors turned away disappointed and repelled by what they saw. General Ulysses Grant (elected American President in 1868) bluffly observed after a visit to the place that Venice would be a 'swell city if only it were drained'. His compatriot, the poet and philosopher Ralph Waldo Emerson, stayed a while in Venice in June 1833, during his first tour of Europe. His wife had recently died and he had resigned as a Pastor of the Unitarian Church. He was thirty, and censorious.

'I am speedily satisfied with Venice,' he wrote in his Journal. 'It is a great oddity, a city for beavers, but, to my thought, a most disagreeable residence. You feel always in prison, and solitary. Two persons may live months in adjoining streets and never meet, for you go about in gondolas, and all the gondolas are exactly alike and the persons within commonly concealed; then there are no newsrooms; except St Mark's Piazza, no place of public resort. It is as if you were always at sea. And though, for a short time, it is very luxurious to lie on the cider-down cushions of your gondola and read or talk or smoke, drawing to, now the cloth-lined

The Bucentaur by Guardi

Austrian bombardment, 1849

shutter, now the Venetian blind, now the glass window, as you please, yet there is always a slight smell of bilgewater about the thing, and houses in the water remind one of a freshet and of desolation, anything but comfort. I soon had enough of it . . .'

The visitor to Venice after 1815 was uneasy too, and found his pity turning into contempt over the continued subjection of the city. When he wrote on the *Constitution of Church and State* (published in 1830) Coleridge attributed the fall of the Republic of Venice to the ossification of the vessels of political power and the loss by the State, in which 'the people were nothing', of all powers of resistance to outside pressure. In contemporary Italy, which except for the ecclesiastical state was all cultivated like a garden, you might find every gift of God – 'only not freedom . . .'

Venice's first martyred heroes of the Risorgimento were Attilio and Emilio Bandiera and Domenico Moro, who were shot at Cosenza in 1844 – betrayed by the British Government – on the orders of the King of Naples after they had attempted to foster an insurrection in Calabria. They are commemorated in Venice in the church of SS. Giovanni e Paolo. In 1848, as rebellions firecrackered across Europe from Paris to Berlin and Vienna and Milan, the Venetians released the imprisoned republican liberals, Daniele Manin and Nicolò Tommaseo, and declared a new Republic under Manin after the Austrian troops were forced to withdraw from Lombardy-Venetia under the pressure of uprisings throughout the peninsular.

At first nearly propelled into a general onslaught on the Austrians, the Italian rulers one by one managed to withdraw from the conflict or stifle their local rebellions and the army of Charles Albert of Piedmont, after some successes, was defeated first at Custoza, then decisively at Novara. Charles Albert abdicated in favour of his son Victor Emmanuel II, who was to become the first ruler of a united Italy. The Venetians had decided to negotiate a union with Piedmont rather than maintain their own independent Republic when Piedmont's armistice with Austria was concluded after Custoza. Manin – who had resigned when the Act of Union was passed – returned to lead Venice against the full onslaught of the Austrian army directed against the city after the battle of Novara.

By April 1849, Venice was beleaguered by 30,000 troops and 150 guns. The defence against blockade, against random bombardment, through a siege of 146 days, was heroic. In August 1849, came the capitulation. Two months later, a 'Provisional Administrative System' imposed from Vienna made Count Radetzky military and civilian Governor of the Kingdom of Lombardy-Venetia, and Milan, Verona and Venice were given separate military governors. A large Austrian garrison had to be

King Victor Emmanuel II

Fête on the Grand Canal

maintained in the Provinces, despite the Emperor's attempts to soften the absolutism of the regime. Venice's resistance to Austrian rule, stiffened by martial successes of 1848, had in the understandably emotional words of Giulio Lorenzetti, 'washed away the blot of ignominy caused by the downfall of her Republic and rehabilitated her honour . . .'

But in 1859 the campaign against Austria by Piedmont and France stopped short of a victory liberating the Venetians and uniting Venice to the rest of Italy. Victor Emmanuel was proclaimed King of Italy in 1861. But the Veneto was freed only in 1866, after the defeat of the Austrians by Prussian forces at Sadowa, and the intervention of the Emperor Napoleon III of France. A plebiscite, by 674,426 votes to 69, joined Venice to the Kingdom of Victor Emmanuel soon after the storming of the Papal States, to become the Kingdom of all Italy, ruled from Rome.

The last days of Austrian government in Venice, and the emotions of the Venetians as they chafed under prolonged alien rule, were dutifully recorded by the American novelist, William Dean Howells, made consul in Venice largely in return for writing a biography to help Abraham Lincoln in his presidential campaign. In his Advertisement written in January 1867 to the second edition of the two volumes of *Venetian Life*, Howells refers to the 'grand and happy events of last summer' – the ceding of Venetia to Italy – but he fancied that in the traits at which he loved most to look, the life of Venice had not so much changed as her fortunes. The two volumes of *Venetian Life* appeared in the 1883 pocket edition series of his works, published in Edinburgh in one shilling volumes, for which I paid £20 in 1977. There is a jaundiced richness in their descriptions of Venice as a city almost in trance, under the clumsy government of the Austrian military. Howells depicts the city as if it were full of ghosts, or marionettes. The Italians and the Austrians are acting their parts on a shabby, broken-down stage, though occasionally we are shown a scene of local life so lively and colourful that time seems to have stopped in the eternal Venetian present. The acting is livened up by the tourists, and chiefly the odd visitors from England.

These come to Venice mainly in the Autumn, Howells tells us, and indeed 'October is the month of the Sunsets and of the English . . .'

'These parties of travelling Englishry are all singularly alike, from the "Pa'ty" travelling alone with his opera-glass and satchel, to the party which fills a gondola with well-cushioned English middle age, ruddy English youth, and substantial England baggage. We have learnt to know them all very well: the father and the mother sit upon the back seat, and their comely girls at the sides and the front. These girls all have the honest cabbage-roses of English health upon their cheeks; they all wear little dowdy English hats, and invariable waterfalls of hair tumble upon their broad English backs. They are coming from Switzerland and Germany, and they are going south to Rome and to Naples, and they always pause at Venice a few days. Tomorrow we shall see them in the Piazza, and at Florian's, and St Mark's, and the Ducal Palace; and the young ladies will cross the Bridge of Sighs, and will sentimentally feed the vagabond pigeons of St Mark which loaf about the Piazza and defile the sculptures. But now our travellers are themselves very hungry, and are more anxious than Americans can understand about the Table-d'hôte of their hotel . . .'

LE PARC ET LE CASINO

Park and casino

Americans do not like these people (as they prate about the civil war), Howells observes; while 'Italians trust and respect private English faith as cordially as they hate public English perfidy . . .' It was the Austrians, of course, not the English tourist with his 'sterling honesty', against whom the Venetians of the 1860s felt the odium and scorn necessary to sustain their self-respect. It might not be a sublime hatred, commented Howells, (it was sometimes mean, lukewarm and selfish), but it was marvellously unanimous and bitter. To be seen in the company of Austrian officers was to be guilty of treason to country and to race. The Italian who married an Austrian severed the dearest ties that bound her to life. The patriotic Comitato Veneto had its secret press, made sure that anniversaries such as the establishment of the Republic in 1848 were publicly celebrated, ensured that no Venetian went to the Piazza when an Austrian band was playing, however exquisite the music. Austrians went to one café, Venetians to another, and only Florian's was common ground, because it was completely cosmopolitan.

The beard was an index to politics: no Austriacante wore the imperial; no Italianissimo shaved it.

In protest against Austrian rule, petards burst in the Cathedral; red, white and green lights were displayed.

The hatred for Austria dated in its full intensity, Howells says, since the defeat of hopes of union with Italy in 1859. '*Bisogno, una volta o l'altra, romper il chiodo*', he quotes: 'sooner or later the nail must be broken . . .' For the present, it is certain that the discontent of the people has its peculiar effect upon the city as the stranger sees its life, vasting a glamour over it all, making it more and more ghostly and sad, and giving it a pathetic charm which I would fain transfer to my pages . . .'

In his pages, Howells caught many of the sudden unexpected charms of the Venetian people and the Venetian scene. He is walking one evening along the Riva degli Schiavoni, towards the formally-planted Public Gardens made by Napoleon. The gardens contain a stable with the only horses in Venice. (This might have made Tchaikovsky think better of Venice which he accused of being dead and gloomy with no horses nor even dogs.) Near them, Howells spies a crowd of sailors, soldiers, countrymen, grey-haired fishermen and ordinary young Venetians 'sitting and lying on the grass, and listening with rapt attention to an old man reclining against a tree. I never saw a manner of sweeter or easier dignity than the speaker's . . . Infinite study could not have taught one northern-born the charm of oratory as this old man displayed it. I listened, and heard that he was speaking Tuscan. Do you guess with what he was enchanting his simple auditors? Nothing less than *Orlando Furioso*. They listened with the hungriest delight, and when Ariosto's interpreter raised his finger and said, "*Disse l'imperatore*," or, "*Orlando disse, Carlomano mio*," they hardly breathed . . .'

During his last year in Venice (Howells is writing seven years after) he lived in the Palazzo Giustiniani and thus enjoyed the privilege of sea-bathing from his own threshold.

'From the beginning of June till far into September all the canals of Venice are populated by the amphibious boys, who clamour about in the brine, or poise themselves for a leap from the tops of bridges, or show their fine, statuesque figures, bronzed by the ardent sun, against the façades of empty palaces, where they hover among the marble sculptures, and meditate a headlong plunge . . . When the tide comes in fresh and strong from the sea the water in the Grand Canal is pure and refreshing; and at these times it is a singular pleasure to leap from one's door-step into the swift current, and spend a half-hour, very informally, among one's neighbours there . . .'

In winter, Howells believes, Venice is the gloomiest place in the world. But he cannot forget even then the city's paradoxical beauty, its constant witness to life and death.

'What summer-delight of other lands could match the beauty of the first Venetian snow-fall which I saw? It had snowed overnight, and in the morning when I woke it was still snowing. The flakes fell softly and vertically through the motionless air, and all the senses were full of languor and repose. It was rapture to lie still, and after a faint glimpse of the golden winged angel on the bell-tower of St Mark's to give indolent eyes solely to the contemplation of the roof opposite, where the snow lay half an inch deep upon the brown tiles . . .'

In Venice, they give the fallen snow no rest . . . 'and now in St Mark's Place the music of innumerable shovels smote upon my ear; and I saw the shivering legion of poverty as it engaged the elements in a struggle for the possession of the Piazza. But the snow continued to fall, and through the twilight of the descending flakes all that weary toil and encounter looked like that weary kind of effort in dreams . . .'

The earnest American consul, peering through the snow, thought how the fantastically lovely Basilica of St Mark's seemed to lose all the stains of decay under the whiteness, as if it had just been built.

As a discerning, always troubled and sometimes inspired literary observer of Venice, Howells was the last of the important amateurs. As the fall of Venice coincided more or less with the rise of Romanticism, so the 'liberation' of Venice coincided with the new cult of the artist, and notably, the exaltation of the novelist. The next American to expend writing skill on the city's powerful psychic and physical attractions would be Henry James, whose fascination with Venice was first stirred by Howells' *Venetian Life*.

Liberated Venice was a magnet too for the new breed of art critics, historians, and men of letters such as John Addington

Symonds, still mostly gentlemen of leisure with literary and scholarly aptitudes, rather than university dons. Among the painters, Whistler, Sickert and Sargent epitomised the Anglo-American vision of Venice in the last decades of the nineteenth century and the first years of this. They went as very self-conscious artists, looking for 'atmosphere', bringing the attitudes and techniques of impressionism to bear on a city valued still mostly for its mysterious combinations of water and sky, light and shade, decline and survival, mud and marble. Venice, so rich in fleeting impressions, its natural scenery so kaleidoscopic, provided perfect material for the increasingly fashionable sketches and watercolours. It was ideal in romantic atmosphere and subject-matter for the painters' exercises which might later be translated into oils. It was ideal for Henry James, with a painter's eye like Shelley. He marks the stage of sensibility when Venice through historical associations and present encounter becomes a vital aesthetic experience that cannot be diminished by acknowledged physical or moral shortcomings. The experience is almost erotic, like falling in love with a person. Its sensuality is heightened by Venice's increasingly rich association with the wilder shores of passion. George Sand conducts there in 1834 her agonising short-lived affair with Alfred de Musset in the Hotel Danieli, then in their lodgings; Venice will provide the scenery for the novels inspired by Chopin. Wagner, who was to die in Venice, staying briefly in 1858–59 at Danieli's, then at the Palazzo Giustiani, finishes scoring Act II in his opera of the great love story of *Tristan und Isolde*. This was, he wrote, 'the highest point that my art has ever reached.'

Henry James' experience of Venice is charged with passion, like the very significant language in which he describes his feelings for the place and the people he met there. The falling in love came in 1881. James had been to Venice a few times before; now, in the words of his marvellous biographer, Leon Edel, as he had taken possession of Rome, Paris and London so 'he took possession of the city of the Doges – and for all his life – in its grandeur and decay . . .'

James passed his thirty-eighth birthday on this visit to Venice, when he stayed on the Riva degli Schiavoni. He would breakfast at Florian's and lunch at Quadri's; walk the streets in the mornings; write in the afternoons; in the evenings, smoke cigarettes

Here is the scene at the chief gondola stand – on the quay under the 2 famous columns –

The English in Venice

and study all the movement of the Grand Canal from the balcony of Ca'Alvisi, an old house occupied by the wealthy American Katherine De Kay Bronson, his friend and Browning's. From London, James wrote to Mrs Bronson that his stay in Venice had taken on the 'semblance of a beautiful dream'. Years later, in *Italian Hours*, he published his memories of the Venice along with other nostalgic tributes to the Italy of his questing youth and middle-age. The several pieces on Venice brood over the past, with mournful intensity. 'Venetian life,' he writes in *The Grand Canal*, 'in the large, old sense, has long since come to an end, and the essential present character of the most melancholy of cities resides simply in its being the most beautiful of tombs.' Venice draws sadness to itself. 'Ever since the *table d'hôte* in *Candide* Venice has been the refuge of monarchs in want of thrones – she wouldn't know herself without her rois en exil . . .' And in Venice we see 'A famous pretender eating the bread of bitterness.'

Two Old Houses and Three Young Women, published in *Italian Hours* and written in 1899, is brimful of echoes and allusions to George Sand and de Musset, to Browning and Ruskin and Wordsworth, strung along a serpentine thread of narrative and

Henry James

historical philosophising, wound round a sentimental idea of Venice as lover, full of favours. 'Dear old Venice has lost her complexion, her figure, her reputation, her self-respect; and yet, with it all, has so puzzlingly not lost a shred of her distinction.'

There was an element of the history of Venice, he said, 'which represents all Europe as having at one time and another revelled or rested, asked for pleasure or for patience there; which gives you the place supremely as the refuge of endless strange secrets, broken fortunes and wounded hearts.'

In *Italian Hours* are litanies of praise for Venice; indeed, James said himself, the time for catalogues was finished but a rhapsody was always in order. In the piece, *Venice: An Early Impression*, the rhapsody is self-consciously wrought with intellectual craft. We are with James as he writes in 1872 and remarks *à propos* of a meeting with a young American painter that 'mere use of one's eyes in Venice is happiness enough'. In Torcello, he has seen 'the handsomest little brats in the world'. And one of them, one small urchin, 'was the most expressively beautiful creature I have ever looked upon . . . I shall always remember with intimate tender conjecture, as the years roll by, this little unlettered Eros of the Adriatic Strand.'

But the most glowing use made by James of his memories of Venice was in his fiction not in his autobiographical reminiscences. An anecdote about Byron and Shelley was the basis for the beautifully plotted story of *The Aspern Papers*, in which descriptions of Venice are integral to the movement of narrative and revelation of character and yet also can be detached from the cunning text to stand as inspired images of the city.

'I spent the late hours either on the water – the moonlights of Venice are famous – or in the splendid square which serves as a vast forecourt to the strange old church of Saint Mark. I sat in front of Florian's café eating ices, listening to music, talking with acquaintances: the traveller will remember how the immense cluster of tables and little chairs stretches like a promontory into the smooth lake of the Piazza. The whole place, of a summer's evening, under the stars and with all the lamps, all the voices and light footsteps on marble – the only sounds of the immense arcade that encloses it – is an open-air saloon dedicated to cooling drinks and to a still finer degustation, that of the splendid impressions received during the day. When I didn't prefer to keep mine to myself there was always a stray tourist, disencumbered of his Baedeker, to discuss them with, or some domesticated painter rejoicing in the return of the season of strong effects. The great basilica, with its low domes and bristling embroideries, the mystery of its mosaic and sculpture, looked ghostly in the tempered gloom, and the sea-breeze passed between the twin columns of the Piazzetta, the lintels of a door no longer guarded, as gently as if a rich curtain swayed there.

'I don't know why it happened that on this occasion I was more than ever struck with that queer air of sociability, of cousinship and family life, which makes up half the expression of Venice. Without streets and vehicles, the uproar of wheels, the brutality of horses, and with its little winding ways where people crowd together, where voices sound as in the corridors of a house, where the human step circulates as if it skirted the angles of furniture and shoes never wear out, the place has the character of an immense collective apartment, in which Piazza San Marco is the most ornamented corner and palaces and churches, for the rest, play the part of great divans of repose, tables of entertainment, expanses of decoration. And somehow the splendid common domicile, familiar, domestic and resonant, also resembles a theatre with its actors clicking over bridges and, in straggling processions, tripping along fondamentas. As you sit in your gondola the footways that in certain parts edge the canals assume to the eye the importance of a stage, meeting it at the same angle, and the Venetian figures, moving to and fro against the battered scenery of their little houses of comedy, strike you as members of an endless dramatic troupe.'

More than once, in his writing of Venice, James mentioned the tourist with his Baedeker. This would be the volume on Northern Italy, with its red cover and gold lettering, of which I have the twelfth edition published in 1903. It has sixty-three pages on Venice. With its eye for the helpful details, practical advice and touches of asperity it is the perfect succinct guide to Venice in the last years of the nineteenth century.

At the railway station gondolas are always waiting and the charge will be one franco or lira during the day, 1.30 at night, with two rowers double fare. Sea-going steamers anchor in the *Bacino di San Marco* and gondolas ply from the steamers to the Piazzetta. The better hotels have electric light, and the Royal Danieli comes first in the list, but there is ample choice of *pensions*, private rooms and furnished apartments, in all of which travellers should make sure their beds are provided with mosquito-curtains.

Travellers should also make sure they do not eat oysters at the many Venetian restaurants, *birrerie* and cafes. They will find the best shops in the *Piazza di San Marco*, the *Merceria*, the *Frezzaria* and the *Salizzada San Moisè*, and several theatres, including the Campo San Fantino, (operas and ballet), the Teatro Rossini, the Teatro Goldoni and the popular Teatro Malibran.

As he goes on the tours and excursions suggested and gazes at buildings and arts treasures described so succinctly in his Baedeker, the visitor should note that in case of doubt, a boy may easily be found to show the way. *Guides* 'are in most cases quite needless, and few, if any, can be trusted to treat their clients fairly and squarely . . .'

An International Art Exhibition is held in Venice every two years, in the Public Gardens. The *Ragattas* held periodically on the Grand Canal 'are characteristic and interesting'. But the Carnival 'which formerly presented a gayer and lighter scene at

Venice than in any other city of Italy, has of late entirely lost its significance'.

One short paragraph in Baedeker, amidst these confident and calm announcements, records a revolution. Since 1888, it reads, the increasing traffic in the canals has been partly met by the small steamboats (*Vaporetti*, also called *Tramways*) of the *Societa di Navigazione Lagunare*.

Venice was linked by steamboat service to Chioggia and Jesolo in 1873. The first steamboat chugged along the Grand Canal in 1881, owned by a French company (the *Compagnie des Bateaux Omnibus de Venise*), after her voyage from the Seine, to start the new internal transport service. The gondoliers went on a forty-eight-hour strike with no chance of success. The steamboats were the first of a series of technological encroachments on Venice that changed the tempo of decline from slow to fast. They began the churning of the water below the surface which very gradually lessened the protection of airlessness and stillness against erosion of the city's wooden foundations. But they also symbolised the prosperity of Venice during the last years of the nineteenth century, fostered by new systems of communications and power, the growth of trade and industry, and the ever-swelling volume of tourists, travelling to the city to see the glory of it.

Ponte Santa Paternina by Moonlight

6 Fanfares and Floods: the Last Glory

Dean Acheson said after Suez that England had lost an empire and not yet found a role. The evaporation of Venice's political importance was also linked to the decay of empire. The enfeeblement of the Venetians' will to power can be pushed back in time as the historian's fancy takes him. Mary McCarthy, for instance, in her sparkling impressionistic essay *Venice Observed* remarks that 'The great deeds of Venetian history were over when her art-history began'. She was in Venice, shrewdly observing and intently listening, in the 1950s. Evelyn Waugh, writing under the heading 'Sinking, Shadowed and Sad – the Last Glory of Europe' told readers of the Daily Mail in 1960 that moralists of the nineteenth century used to draw comparisons between London and Venice ('mercantile, maritime and imperial') and to warn Londoners that they too might decline if they gave way to luxury and ostentation. But economic ineptitude put paid to luxury and the real lesson was very different, Waugh reflected. And if 'every museum in the New World were emptied, if every famous building in the Old World were destroyed and only Venice saved, there would be enough there to fill a full lifetime with delight. Venice, with all its complexity and variety, is in itself the greatest surviving work of art in the world.'

Countess Cicogna, talking with animation to Lord Snowdon when he was photographing the city in 1972, said that since the fall of the Republic, there had not been found another function for Venice. 'This was the capital city of an empire. It is difficult to change the capital city of an empire into a self-sufficient object . . .'

While Venice stayed a city-state, maritime still and imperial, though neutral, there remained the possibility of political regeneration. When the Republic chose abdication, it grew impotent first under occupation, then under the embrace of a unified unconcerned Italy. 'What do other Italians think of the Venetians?' I asked a friend from Turin recently. 'We don't think of them,' he replied.

Not only did the old diminished role vanish, the past was increasingly turned into the merely picturesque, with Venetian galleys like painted boats on painted seas. Historians exploded some of the antique myths, about the Bridge of Sighs, for example, as the cross-over to death. But the truth behind all the myths – of old Venetian integrity as well as Venetian terror – was rarely sought. The serious study of Venetian history was largely diverted into a brilliant pastiche of set-pieces. Meanwhile, the Venetians of the twentieth century seem hardly to have spoken, except in their own dialogue and voting-booths to each other. Political events, intruding into Venice, have been transformed there into tragi-comedy. At least Napoleon had paid the Venetian Republic the tribute of hate: '*Je ne veux plus ni inquisition, ni Livre d'Or; ce sont des institutions des siècles de barbarie* . . .' ['I want no more inquisition, or Golden Book; they are the institutions of centuries of barbarism . . .']

The Vatican has been called (by Professor Denys Hay) the 'nearest thing the Italians have ever got to a "national" institution' and three Popes have ascended to the Papal throne during this century after being Patriarchs of Venice. For the rest of 'national' Italy, the Venetians have occasionally provided the backcloth for demonstrations of patriotic fervour rather than acted prominently in the politics of central power.

Gabriele d'Annunzio, the sallow, sensuous poet of Italy's self-glorification, used Venice as the springboard for his sudden hurtlings into heroic action against the Austrian enemy in 1915. He arrived at the Danieli in the summer, finding an embattled city from which the tourists of the Belle Epoque, so rich and aristocratic and sparkling, had receded in a whoosh. A self-entitled *Comandante*, d'Annunzio bombed Trieste and Trent from the air with flags and paper rhetoric; sped by motor-boat into Austrian harbours to torpedo enemy shipping; zoomed out of the sky over Zara, in Dalmatia, to launch the message that the Lions of St Mark's would roar again in that city; lost an eye by being thrown against his own machine-gun; and won a silver medal. He stayed and made love in the Casetta Rossa, a palace which the Austrians tried to bomb but in vain – hitting the Morisini instead. In his novel *Il Fuoco*, d'Annunzio left the scandalous record of his affair with Eleonora Duse, depicted as withered and erotic, and a vividly coloured verbal map of Venice, contoured so as to suggest exotic comparisons with the voluptuousness of an older woman, as the lovely city existed at the turn of the century. Venice was the 'terrible temptress'. Venice, d'Annunzio used like a whore for his literary declamations. For d'Annunzio's flamboyant military escapades, the city happened to be there, but ill-matched to his imperial Roman revivalism and incipiently fascist course.

Adolf Hitler and Benito Mussolini incongruously agreed to Venice as the place for their first meeting, in June 1934. The talks were inconclusive, full of hilarious moments. Mussolini stayed at the historic spot of Strà in the most splendid of the villas of the Brenta which had been built in the eighteenth century for the ducal Pisanis, bought by Napoleon for his viceroy, taken by the Italian Crown and was now deserted and ill-equipped for the encounter. There was no crockery. Hitler – met on arrival by Mussolini at his car's driving-wheel – lodged in the royal suite at the Grand Hotel; and because of mosquitoes, most of the inconclusive discussions took place in Venice where the German Chancellor, wearing soft hay and mackintosh, heard the Duce, in flamboyant uniform, with dagger, orating before a Venetian crowd.

Mussolini's wife, Rachele, recalled being told by him: 'Hitler talked a lot, after stumbling over his words, and put forward some wild ideas. He hasn't much self-control. Our meeting came to nothing.' (But their second meeting, September 1937, in Germany, laid the foundations of the 'Pact of Steel'.) After lunching at the Villa Pisani on 14 June, Hitler did some sightseeing in Venice. On 15 June, he lunched on the Lido, at the Alberoni fort. It was that afternoon he heard Mussolini's public speech, watching from a balcony in Piazza San Marco. He

Eleonora Duse

returned to Germany to murder his own SA followers. In his 'Table Talk' (5 July, 1942), Hitler said: 'The Venetian Republic affords an excellent example of how successful a state-directed economy can be. For 500 years the price of bread in Venice never varied, and it was left to the Jews with their predatory motto of Free Trade to wreck this stability . . .' In 1943, after the rescue of Mussolini from the Badaglio Government and his restoration as puppet dictator, in the plans for the surrender to Greater Germany of Trieste, Istria and the South Tyrol, provision was considered also for the incorporation of Venetia in the Reich.

James Morris, in his *Venice*, says that he heard from a custodian of the Doge's Palace that Hitler admired it, and also wandered in the early hours around Venice by himself.

In Mussolini's Italy, Venice stayed subdued. Ciano, who was one of the Duce's numerous entourage when he met Hitler in 1934, left some bleak impressions of wartime Venice in his diary. For 29 December, 1940: 'In Venice I saw little and can say little about how the people feel. Some degrees below freezing, and the lagoons are covered with ice; such being the case, the Venetians are unwilling to interest themselves in politics.' For 15 December, 1941: 'Venice was sad, empty, tired. Never have I seen it so squalid. Empty hotels, deserted streets. Fog. Misery. Darkness. I have only vague memories of the Venice of the other

Hitler meets Mussolini

Gabriele d'Annunzio

war, but it was not at all like this. If nothing else, there was the sentimental attraction of the front-line city.' For 28 August, 1942: 'In Venice. A visit to the biennial exhibition . . . We had two painters who are important: De Chirico and Sciltian . . .' Then, for 23 December, 1943, an entry that quickens the pulse as Ciano, writing in prison in Verona, tries to fix the responsibility of men and governments for Italy's tragedy: '. . . on 16 June (1941) I was with von Ribbentrop in Venice discussing the inclusion of Croatia in the Tripartite Pact. The world was filled with rumour about an impending act of aggression against the Soviets, despite the fact that the ink was not yet dry on the friendship pact signed between the Germans and the Soviets. I asked my Axis colleague about it in a gondola while we were going from the hotel Danieli to a dinner party given by Count Volpi in his palace . . .' Ribbentrop's reply was: '. . . if we attack, the Russia of Stalin will be erased from the map within eight weeks.'

The Axis forces in Italy surrendered in May 1945, after bloody fighting by the Eighth Army to drive the Germans back beyond the River Po and the collapse of the resistance that had been expected on the River Adige – the Venetian Line. Venice – and Padua – had been captured on 29 April. In the conflict, Italian partisans played a ferocious part. One of their leaders, the author and journalist Peter Tumiati (my former colleague on the *Financial Times* and long-standing friend) recalls the element of farce in the freeing of Venice. It was raining. The walls of the city were scrawled with the slogans.

163

'Bruno suddenly appeared the day after the liberation claiming to have been a partisan leader and as such he was accepted; when the carabinieri arrived in Venice they arrested him. The British municipal commissioner came to me to enlist my support against the move by the carabinieri. More or less with these words he said: "It is absolutely intolerable: the first thing the carabinieri do on getting here is to arrest a partisan leader." We went to the carabinieri and told them what we thought of them. When we had finished the carabinieri major asked us to go to the prison with him. We went there and he showed us the prison register: at the time of the liberation of Venice Bruno was in jail serving his third or fourth sentence for burglary. He had got out that day and immediately posed as a partisan leader!'

Peter, half-English, half-Italian, a man of stature and humour, told me the story ironically in his Roman apartment in the Città Antica, before my last visit to Venice, when my mind was full of literary Venice, busy over the fascination of the city which has triumphed over occupation, war, fascism, periods of swift physical decline and natural disaster to re-assert its hold on the imagination of the writer. In this century, ever more tourists have flocked there and so have the novelists who have marvellously deepened understanding of the city's unique grace in being able to stimulate the creative spirit. They have fused the natural and man-made beauty and mystery of Venice with their own constructions, so that in the great works, the city loved and penetrated becomes one flesh with their fiction. The novels and stories are enriched by the now incredibly rich tradition, the awareness of the ghosts of previous writers meditating on the same material provided by the stones and water and people of Venice. Sometimes, the writers meet the living past.

John Cowper Powys, on holiday in Venice in 1912, hires a gondola with his companions.

'Somewhere down by the Rialto, in a very crowded and narrow canal, we encountered, as we were propelled through the water, a floating equipage that resembled the barge of Cleopatra, or perhaps I ought to say that ship, so often delineated in Greek vase paintings, that carried the great god Dionysus on his triumphant voyage. This other gondola whose high ornamental poop collided with our own, was actually covered with the most wonderful skins of leopards and lynxes and it was handled by a Being who might very well have passed for the Faun of Prax-iteles. In the stern, lying on a leopard's skin, was a personage who, as I learnt later, was one of the most whimsical writers and one of the most beguiling men of the great works . . .'

It was the year before the death in Venice of this most whimsical writer, Baron Corvo, Frederick Rolfe, the 'strange tormented spirit' whose story is best followed in A. J. A. Symonds' lucid masterpiece of biographical detection *The Quest for Corvo*. Rolfe collapsed in the streets of Venice in the bitter cold of March, leaving both grim and glittering images of Venice: the under-world letters about his homosexual swoonings and seductions, the richly brocaded maddened satire, *The Desire and Pursuit of the Whole*, from which – the bucket can be dipped and dipped again – one quotation brings Corvo's Venice, where he indulged the lust of the eye, in motion before us, through the observations of Nicholas Crabbe, Rolfe himself.

'Every kind of athletic association was represented in The Giar-dinetto Reale: the glorious Bucintoro in black and white, the valorous Querini (who scoop all prizes) in white and blue, row-ing clubs, football clubs, bicycle clubs, walking clubs, fencing clubs, gymnastic clubs, companies from schools and palestre, a battalion from the Technical Institute in quaint green, red-slashed medieval berettas copied from the university of Padova. White armlets with the legend *"Pro Calabria e Sicilia"* were being served out to all. Bands were proving brazen. Money-collectors clanked tins or rattled wooden boxes. Shoals of barks, topi, balesane, pupparini, barchette, cavalline, floated by the terrace steps. And, every now and then, a squadron got its route, and marched away in the sharp sunlight, with music to move and enliven the merciful.

'Venetian courtesy avoided offering burthens to an English-man, and Crabbe had to insist on his right to work. "If His Sioria would repeat his labour of yesterday –" was insinuated. He looked round for a third oarsman, with a view of accelerating speed. A tiny coxswain of the Bucintoro volunteered, Hebrew, shrill-voiced as a jay, active as an ape, with a lovely thirteenth-century Hebrew name, William Grace-of-God, Memi Graziadei. Crabbe looked him over, vivacious gait and expression, haughty little nose, devilish little eyes, already-darkened little upper lip, and nodded assent.'

John Cowper Powys, describes his encounter with Baron Corvo in his thick-textured, mind-teasing *Autobiography*. In Corvo's *The Desire and Pursuit of the Whole*, Nicholas Crabbe pursues the girl–boy figure of Zilda. In Powys' book, the latter is strangely matched by the real-life figure of Frances Gregg, a beautiful and spirited American married to a close friend of Powys, loved by the two of them and by John's brother Llewelyn. Venice, recalled the dominant figure of this amorously odd quartet, had always been to him much more the Venice of the equivocal Henry James than of the lusty Byron. It was the place that 'alone of all mortal places answers to the vision that precedes realisation, the thickly-charged atmosphere of the coiners of phrases, the atmosphere projected by the scribblers on paper . . .' Constipated (by the sour white wine of Florence, he claimed), Powys confessed that his wretched physical state made a deeper impression on his mind than 'the pink feet of the pigeons of St Mark or the tables of that hospitable café past which all the idlers of Europe drift'. But the chief memory was of the kind of sexual frenzy that Venice can induce, caught in the naive details of an escapade that sounds both poignant and absurd and of a piece with Venetian moods.

'There was some small kind of a war going on at that epoch between Italy and some other country; and I dare say our appearance when we escorted this girl about Venice was odd and striking. At any rate we were disembarking from our gondola one day not far from the Bridge of Sighs when we found ourselves surrounded by an imposing band of officials. It was explained to us that we were under arrest. "This," they said, indicating our friend, "is a feminine one; yes? no?"

'Llewelyn whispered to me that it was just as if they had caught a hatful of trespassing butterflies and discovered among them, by the markings under her wings, a fine female specimen. This is the only occasion so far in my life when I have been in the hands of the police; and really when we were all led into some upper-chamber, and made to stand in a row before a grave personage at a table, I felt as if the chief of the "Volentia Army" were being treated as he had so often treated our little nurse from Berkshire, in that robber's roof-attic at Rothesay House!

Patriotic illumination of the Rialto

'Our Venetian address was carefully taken down – an hotel on the Lido – and then came the question of our home address. Not one of us had a "card" except Llewelyn, and he had, by some chance, one of my father's. Never had those familiar words: "Rev. C. F. Powys, Montacute Vicarage, Somerset" sounded so out of place; but the Venetian official chuckled a good deal and handed the card to one of his subordinates. We caught the word "padre" exchanged between them accompanied by what no doubt was a sly commentary on the progenitive capacity of priests in England. An official at once hurried off to the Lido to verify our story, and once again Llewelyn saved us; for, after his fashion, he had so courted, cajoled, caressed, and generally bewitched our landlady, that the woman led the emissary to think that our social position at home, in spite of the padre's card, was a tremendous one, and that we were only behaving in our accustomed manner, like so many Milords Byron.

'But my excitement during those wild Venetian days rose to a pitch that I have never known before or since.'

Powys had intended to travel to Venice, he remembers, by train from France: 'by that express from Paris that the hero of Proust's Book must have taken on the occasion when he felt that famous unevenness in the paving-stones of St Mark's, which, like that mouthful of the Madeleine dips in camomile-tea, gave him one of his immortality-proving ecstasies . . .'

Proust's experience of Venice indeed exemplifies the changed sensibilities of the literate visitor to the city. Proust's way is neither romantic nor realistic; the writer observes and describes as accurately as possible what he sees, positively accepting that it is susceptible to his own feelings and mood of a particular time. In *A La Recherche du Temps Perdu*, Venice, or rather the idea that Proust forms of Venice, is neither prop nor backcloth simply but an essential element of the novel, involved almost as if a person.

Proust will say, when recalling his first visit to Venice, that he found 'my dream has become – incredibly but quite simply – my *address*!' He was there with his mother, staying at the Danieli, in 1900, testing what he saw against the promise contained in the pages of Ruskin, whose writing he had wonderingly explored and would mine for gold to gild his own pages.

Wherever the writer and his mother travelled, observes George Painter in his superb two-volume biography of Marcel Proust, they invariably were to be found at the best hotel. So in Venice it was the one at the top of Baedeker's list, the Danieli, and from there in the mornings Proust would set forth to visit churches and palaces described by Ruskin; in the afternoons, sit at Florian's in the Piazza of San Marco, eating *granita*, the honey-combed ice, and watching the pigeons. On a visit to Padua, Proust saw and retained as images for use in his novel the figures of Giotto's frescoes. Proust's second visit to Venice in the same year of 1900, his biographer suggests, may have been to explore again the novel aspects of art and nature which it offered, as well as to wander alone in search of working-class girls, and 'sinister enchantments' such as Byron and Corvo found.

For the hero-narrator of *A La Recherche du Temps Perdu* – the first version of which was completed in 1912 – Venice provides one of the main geographical 'settings' of his Odyssey through time. He is tormented since boyhood (when a visit promised by his father had to be cancelled) by the yearning to see the city. At length, he goes there with his mother.

*Spiral stairs at the
Palazzo Contarini*

Proust's own nostalgia for Venice after 1900 and his experiences there in May and October 1900, artistically shaped and sharpened, are woven into the fabric of *A La Recherche*. The incident of the uneven flagstones over which Proust stumbled as he was crossing a courtyard, summoning images of Venice to his mind, like the eating of the madeleine in childhood, at the end of the novel releases as it did in real life from unconscious memory the messages of the past that renew all the past in the present. As described in *Time Regained* – the last chapter – the stumble in the courtyard of the Guermantes' mansion brings back the vision of its Baptistry of St Mark's and all Venice with it. In turn, Proust's Venice as re-created in *A La Recherche* affects the atmosphere and the appearance of the real Venice for those who know Proust and the city. This is *Proust*'s Venice, timeless, in Scott-Moncrieff's translation:

'After dinner, I went out by myself, into the heart of the enchanted city where I found myself wandering in strange regions like a character in the arabian nights. It was very seldom that I did not, in the course of my wanderings, hit upon some strange and spacious piazza of which no guide-book, no tourist had ever told me.

169

'I had plunged into a network of little alleys, *calli*, dissecting in all directions by their ramifications the quarter of Venice isolated between a canal and the lagoon, as if it had crystallised along these innumerable, slender, capillary lines. All of a sudden, at the end of one of those little streets, it seemed as though a bubble had occurred in the crystallised matter. A vast and splendid campo of which I could certainly never, in this network of little streets, have guessed the importance, or even found room for it, spread out before me flanked with charming palaces silvery in the moonlight. It was one of those architectural wholes towards which, in any other town, the streets converge, lead you and point the way. Here it seemed to be deliberately concealed in a labyrinth of alleys, like those palaces in oriental tales to which mysterious agents convey by night a person who, taken home again before daybreak, can never again find his way back to the magic dwelling which he ends by supposing that he visited only in a dream.

'On the following day I set out in quest of my beautiful nocturnal piazza, I followed *calli* which were exactly like one another and refused to give me any information, except such as would lead me farther astray. Sometimes a vague landmark which I seemed to recognise led me to suppose that I was about to see appear, in its seclusion, solitude and silence, the beautiful exiled piazza. At that moment, some evil genie which had assumed the form of a fresh *calle* made me turn unconsciously from my course, and I found myself suddenly brought back to the Grand Canal. And as there is no great difference between the memory of a dream and the memory of a reality, I ended by asking myself whether it was not during my sleep that there had occurred in a dark patch of Venetian crystallisation that strange interruption which offered a vast piazza flanked by romantic palaces, to the meditative eye of the moon.'

All novelists who choose Venice for their setting, all the poets, painters, film-makers, must even if unconsciously reflect in their representation the layer of timelessness and nostalgia laid on the city's image by Proust, and perhaps equally or more the layer of melancholy and pessimism imposed by Thomas Mann. *Der Tod in Venedig* (*Death in Venice*) first published in 1913 tells the story of the ageing writer, Gustave Aschenbach, whose life has been utterly spent on artistic creation, who suddenly in a Venice where there is death in the air falls victim to his suppressed anarchic and erotic impulses under the assault on his mind of a beautiful boy, Tadzio. The film *Death in Venice*, using the music of Mahler, on whom Mann supposedly based the character of Aschenbach, projects a weird, almost surreal Venice of fantasy and mistiness; but with Mann's book, we are still in the time of the Belle Epoque; the images, like those of Henry James in *The Turn of the Screw*, are like the writing – hard and clear, sharp-edged as intellect. Venice is almost personified as it plays its key part in the drama. Aschenbach is shortly to make his fatal decision that he will not leave Venice for all its menace and corruption. He takes the vaporetto to Venice from the Lido, and after taking tea in the Piazza San Marco, starts a customary walk.

'There was a hateful sultriness in the narrow streets. The air was so heavy that all the manifold smells wafted out of houses, shops, and cook-shops – smells of oil, perfumery, and so forth – hung low, like exhalations, not dissipating. Cigarette smoke seemed to stand in the air, it drifted so slowly away. Today the crowd in these narrow lanes oppressed the stroller instead of diverting him. The longer he walked, the more was he in tortures under

171

that state, which is the product of the sea air and the sirocco and
which excites and enervates at once. He perspired painfully. His
eyes rebelled, his chest was heavy, he felt feverish, the blood
throbbed in his temples. He fled from the huddled, narrow
streets of the commercial city, crossed many bridges, and came
into the poor quarter of Venice. Beggars waylaid him, the canals
sickened him with their evil exhalations. He reached a quiet
square, one of those that exist at the city's heart, forsaken of God
and man; there he rested awhile on the margin of a fountain,
wiped his brow, and admitted to himself that he must be gone.

'For the second time, and now quite definitely, the city proved
that in certain weathers it could be directly inimical to his health.
Nothing but sheer unreasoning obstinacy would linger on, hop-
ing for an unprophesiable change in the wind. A quick decision
was in place. He could not go home at this stage, neither summer
nor winter quarters would be ready. But Venice had not a
monopoly of sea and shore: there were other spots where these
were to be had without the evil concomitants of lagoon and
fever-breeding vapours. He remembered a little bathing-place

not far from Trieste of which he had had a good report. Why not go thither: At once, of course, in order that this second change might be worth the making.

'He resolved, he rose to his feet and sought the nearest gondola-landing, where he took a boat and was conveyed to San Marco through the gloomy windings of many canals, beneath balconies of delicate marble traceries flanked by carven lions; round slippery corners of wall, past melancholy façades with ancient business shields reflected in the rocking water. It was not too easy to arrive at his destination, for his gondolier, being in league with various lace-makers and glass-blowers, did his best to persuade his fare to pause, look, and be tempted to buy. Thus the charm of this bizarre passage through the heart of Venice, even while it played upon his spirit, yet was sensibly cooled by the predatory commercial spirit of the fallen queen of the seas.'* Ezra Pound, who in the 1920s condemned the 'enervating' influence of Proust and looked sympathetically towards d'Annunzio as a writer and man of action, leaves a sunnier image,

* From the translation by H. T. Lowe-Porter.

in his early poetry, of the fallen queen of Mann and Proust. He stayed there, above a bakery at the Ponte San Vio, then in the Calle dei Frati, a poor young poet whom Venice inspired. Venice (where he published *A Lume Spento*, from which many poems survive into his collected works), believes Pound's biographer, Noel Stock, may well have been a turning-point for his poetry. In the poem '*Alma Sol Veneziae*', he wrote:

> *Thou that has given me back*
> *Strength for the journey,*
> *Thou that hast given me*
> *Heart for the journey*
> *O sun venezian . . .*

He was to be buried in Venice, not far from Corvo's coffin, on the island of San Michele.

In the Great War of 1914–1918, the city was turned over to the military, evacuated by most of the civilians, and fortified as a base against the Austrians. In England, it earned literary praise chiefly for the Arsenal which, said a contributor to the Pro Italia Committee's *Book of Italy*, provided a superb historical example of organisation for war. (And, in the sixteenth century, of extraordinarily sophisticated management and control systems, the management writer John Diebold was to add in a business lecture in 1978.)

But the influence of the city on literature, after bursts of creative inter-action during the nineteenth and early part of the twentieth century, dwindled miserably during the period of fascist rule in Italy. So, from the First World War till after the Second, did the flood of books on Venice. Today tourists swarm seasonally to Venice but the old Anglo-American community that used to live there permanently or for months at a stretch is reduced to a handful. Cecil Roberts evocatively conveys the flavour of one kind of society that even so lingered on into the post-war years, in his reminiscences of *The Pleasant Years* (Hodder and Stoughton, 1974). He is writing about the English in Venice in 1949, and the years before.

'I arrived in Venice and found many friends at the Hotel Gritti, on the Grand Canal: Mrs Crane, the Duff Coopers, Lord Robert Cecil and his wife, and a tireless American benefactor of St Mark's, Mrs Truxton Beale (her seal is now marked by a plaque

*Palazzo
Contarini-
Polignac*

inside the basilica). What fun life was in Venice, what Goldoni-like intrigues, what Guardianesque moments in the pigeon-cluttered Piazza, what strange combinations of people and history! The Robilants gave parties in the salon of their Palazzo Mocenigo on the Grand Canal, where Byron had kept his mistresses and read to Shelley the first Canto of Don Juan. One afternoon we went by gondola, with Mrs Crane and Sir Kenneth and Lady Clark, on the track of a reputed Titian in the studio of Italico Brass. The International PEN, holding a conference, gave a ball at the Palazzo Rezzonico, in the great ballroom with its trompe l'oeil by Tiepolo, where Robert Browning had lain in state in 1889, prior to transition to Westminster Abbey.

'One day I lunched at the Palladian Villa Malcontenta, with its high-columned portico and the semi-erotic frescoes that my host, restoring the villa, had uncovered . . .

'This was my twenty-first visit to Venice since 1922. There had been changes but many old friends were there. What memories were evoked! For a quarter of a century I had known the Garden of Eden, that island tethered to the Giudecca, with its long sea-wall looking south down the lagoon, and its immense garden of vines, cypresses and roses. It was the home of Princess Aspasia, widow of King Alexander of Greece, killed by a monkey's bite. Dear, sad woman. A ridiculous rumour had grown up

175

that she possessed the evil eye, and suspicious people made the traditional sign with their fingers to ward off the danger in her glance. She was still beautiful, if not with the beauty Compton Mackenzie, seeing her before her marriage, had recorded in his Greek Memories. Her home, and this lovely garden, had taken its name from the Englishman, Mr Eden, who had created it on the Giudecca. It held ghosts for me. Here in the twenties young Derek Mond and my young Lucien Reid and his sister had played with the Princess's little daughter, Alessandra. Both boys had perished in the flower of their youth, in the Second World War . . .'

Out of Venice and the English, L. P. Hartley created a fine novel, rich in symbols and steeped in dreams, which contains some of the most sensitive descriptions of the city, closely-fitted to story line and characterisation. The book is *Eustace and Hilda*, published in 1947, as the last novel of his trilogy, looking back to vanished worlds. The opening scene shows Lady Nelly Staveley stepping out into the Piazza San Marco, Henry James' 'drawing room' of Europe. Venice beautifully suits as the setting for Hartley's drama of the tension in man's own soul between good and evil. Specifically, the Feast of the Redeemer, observed in Venice, symbolised the final salvation of the hero. But here is one of Hartley's scrupulously observed studies of Venice, which leads to a climactic episode when the face of Christ, and a crown of thorns, are traced in fireworks.

'The place was indeed well chosen, and Silvestro had disposed the gondola so that the reclining ladies and their upright escorts opposite had only to turn their heads to see the church of the Redentore. Silvery and expectant, looking larger than by day, it met them almost full-face. Behind them the moon sent a track across the water which, continually broken by the dark forms of boats, made nevertheless a ribbon of light between them and the church where it gloriously terminated; and on their left the bridge, which had also gained in impressiveness since the morning, made an angle with the line of moonlight, a slender black-and-white V whose apex was the church. In both directions people were crowding across the bridge. Eustace could hear their voices and the shuffle of their feet, and see them descend, slow-moving and tiny, on to the space in front of the great church. Up

176

the steps they went until the shadow of the high doorway, thrown inwards, effaced them as they crossed the threshold.

'Beyond the noise of voices, the snatches of music, the swinging of paper lanterns, the tilting and dipping of sterns and bows, the church in its grey immensity stood motionless and silent. Now that Eustace was growing accustomed to the light he saw that the façade was faintly flood-lit by the lamps at its base, a wash of gold had crept along the silver. Yet how stern were the uncompromising straight lines, drawn like a diagram against the night; how intimidating the shadows behind the buttresses which supported roof and dome. The church drew his eyes to it with a promise which was almost threatening, so powerfully did it affect his mind.

'They had finished supper, they had eaten the duck, the mulberries and the mandarins, the traditional fare of the feast, and were sitting with their champagne glasses in front of them on the white tablecloth when the first rocket went up. Eustace heard the swish like the hissing intake of a giant breath, and his startled nerves seemed to follow its flight. Then with a soft round plop the knot of tension broke, and the core of fiery green dissolved into single stars which floated down with infinite languor towards the thousands of upturned faces. A ripple of delight went through the argosy of pleasure-seekers. Night rushed back into the heavens; the moon, now low down behind the houses, tried to resume her sway; but Nature's spell was broken, everyone was keyed up for the next ascent. Soon it came, bursting into an umbrella of white and crimson drops that almost reached the water before they died, and were reflected in the tablecloth. For a time, at irregular intervals, single rockets continued to go up; then there was a concerted swish, a round of popping as though scores of corks were being drawn, and arc upon arc of colour blotted out the sky. The infant stars burst from their matrix and, still borne aloft by the impetus of their ascent, touched the summit of their flight, brushed the floor of Heaven and then fell back appeased.'

Elsewhere, Hartley's ability to describe the sheer, breathless beauty of Venice is as fine as Shelley's. We can smell the place and hear its sounds. He loves women in their complexity, judging by the delicacy and frankness with which he portrays the bodies and

177

Palazzo Balbi

minds of his female characters, the *grande dame* or the loving slut, and he tells us more about Venetian women than most other literary observers have done. (Though Hemingway bundles a woman before us, along with some brilliant colour-strokes of Venetian scenery and bar-life, in *Across the River and Into the Trees*; and Alice Meynell, in her 'Wayfaring' Essays, written at the turn of the century, lightly sketched the Venetian girls, wearing black, eddying through the streets, with straight dark hair, laughing like bells and utterly composed. 'None of their painters,' she said, 'seem to be aware of that peculiar reserve, nor of the look they all wear as conscious Venetians. Theirs is the incomparable city . . .')

Guardian of the Palazzo Santarato, Hans Habe's seventy-four-year-old Signora reminds her visitor, Dario, 'for a moment of Venetian glass, but glass which in the twentieth century had taken on the bluntness of the age. Clad in black, spreading her wide skirt over the armchair like the dying swan on the stage floor she looked like a dark ballerina. But she was not always a dying swan; when she moved, she was more of a marching dragon, the quiet house loud with her steps . . .'

And the quiet house epitomises the Venetian palazzo, one of the instantly felt symbols of Venetian civic solidarity, beauty, comfort and art. Anna-Maria Santarato's palazzo has a garden to the landward side, behind a high wall. There are trees and a patch of green and waterless fountain.

'The ground floor is empty. Spices and bales of cloth, sacks full of flour and crates with crystal, were once stored here. Some time later gondolieri would wait here for orders, dozing, gambling, swearing. Now it is a cave, wet stones to slip on, walls sweating with cold, the shadows inert. There are unused marble stairs, like a house-painter's ladder left behind; and right beside them a wooden staircase leading up to a rather ugly letter-box.

'On the first floor everything, or nearly everything, remains as it was. The drawing-room is suspended above the Canal Grande like a free balloon, with its columns, paintings, statues, show-cases, stucco-work, damask, ascending angels, falling curtains, cool marble, glowing glass. But in the small dining-room next door, only every third lamp is lit, the engravings are pock-marked, the loose frames have turned the paintings into reliefs.

Palazzo Bernardo

Storm and flood

The corridors are dark, and poverty creeps through the cracks of the locked kitchen door. The bedrooms on the second floor are the stage sets of a forgotten theatre. The two guest-rooms are bleakly superfluous. Only the bedroom with the canopy, fashioned after a gondola, with the gold-lacquered tables and dolls' chairs and frills, presents a lace curtain dropped over the dusty stage.'

The air of menace in Habe's *Palazzo* is created both by the struggle between good and evil in the intentions of Venetians themselves and by the threat from outside, the ancient threat reinforced by the forces of the modern industrial world. Throughout their history, the Venetians fought the Turks, the Genoese, the Imperialists, at times (as during the War of Cambrai) it seemed, all the world in arms, sometimes with guile and sly neutrality, sometimes with astounding counter-violence, keeping the balance, grasping the space to breathe, striking for more. But throughout history, simultaneously ally and foe, lover and assassin, the sea has been the element of highest danger.

Venice's death-warrant was as if signed by its location – abandoned Torcello a permanent *memento mori* – but with execution indefinitely postponed. The city has always been sinking into the water on which it was built; always frayed by the salty air; always subject to the dreaded potential disaster of a combination, like four horses of the Apocalypse, of high tides, thrusting marine currents, the fierce *sirocco*, and the oscillation of the Adriatic sea. In this century, the dangers of swift disaster and of death by attrition have been alarmingly magnified by the expansion of industry on the lagoon shores at *Marghera*, drawing off population, polluting the water and the air, cracking the foundations of the lagoon, rocking the age-old equilibrium between earth and water.

In Hans Habe's novel, in the warm company of flesh-and-blood Venetians, we are abruptly assailed by the great flood (storming over most northern Italy) that swept into the city in the fateful year of 1966. Habe points up the arguments against 'progress' – and there is, there always is, another side with arguments to deploy in favour of industrialisation and employment – through the clashes of his characters. Similarly, but with the truth of a novelist's descriptive insight, he dramatises the flood.

'From the direction of the Lido the brown waves surged, in soiled armour they stormed the city. The seagulls sitting on the poles – which mark the way for the ships – fled across the sea. They flew high. The waves ground up the sand-banks, the bareni, and carried off towards the city what had accumulated on them during sunny days: boards, refuse, crates, broken prams, discarded dolls, torn dresses, snapped oars. Briefly they broke on the island of San Giorgio Maggiore; the dark training vessel lying in the ducal bacino was attacked from the sea side; white sails were lowered to the water, like the flag of the vanquished before the enemy.

'Then the floods swept over the pier and hurled themselves against the pillars of the Palazzo Ducale. They locked their teeth in the heels of the columns, jumped up at them, tore at their clothing. All the shops in the Piazza San Marco were closed, within an hour the iron sliding shutters had come rattling down in front of the shop windows, one big rumble, a brief close-range action under the arcades. Courageous helpers had erected the narrow bridges of boards on their platforms, but the gangplanks had already sunk beneath the surface, and their timbers floated away. If the frightened tourists behind the windows of their hotel-rooms had known more about Venice, they would have realised that the golden clouds of Venetian baroque are like the raging foam which was dashing up the pillars and shop-windows of the colonnades. The more hard-pressed the sea, the greater its wrath.

'The gondolieri had not waited for the howl of sirens, the whisper of instinct was enough. The poles where they tied their boats had become unsafe, a forest of defoliated trees shaken by the wind. Across the piazzetta, past the ducal palace and towards St Mark's Church, the gondolieri were rowing, still careful not to obstruct each other. They fastened the gondolas to the four-armed lanterns with their roots in stone, like cowboys tethering their horses outside the saloons; only they could not walk inside for a drink, the gondolas would have gone wild and torn loose.

'The Signora had experienced this so often that she saw the city before her, and what her eyes could not see, was blown to her by the wind. Initially, she heard the rumbling sea only from afar, but the wind had preceded the waves, it whistled through the Canal, the window-panes rattled, the beams were creaking. The winged Fortuna on the golden globe of the maritime customs office, which looks more like Mercury, God of the merchants and the thieves, than the Goddess of Fortune, was rotating frantically. Police boats with policemen in summery white were driving back and forth, once in a while a red fireboat appeared, called up by the rage of one element, failing before the other.

'Without warning, not content with their conquest of the ducal palace, the Piazzetta, the Riva degli Schiavoni, and St Mark's Square, the waves invaded the side-canals. The lions of the Palazzo dei Leoni had quenched their thirst at the feet of the columns; now their nostrils, their eyes disappeared, at last their manes were engulfed. Red-white, blue-white, violet-white poles fell, like drunken sailors going overboard. On the Fondamenta dell'Osmarin the water whisked away a street-painter's easel; red, blue and green dissolved into brown. Some fruit vendors

Flood in San Marco

and fishmongers had not saved their wares in the market early enough. Eggs toppled into the water, oranges sank, only the dead fish fell back in their element. The Church of San Lorenzo echoed the waves' maniacal laughter at catching a painting here just as it was being saved, and tearing it from its hiding-place. In the court of the Palazzo degli Orfei they met with unexpected resistance: after the last flood the garden was wildly overgrown, bushes and thistle hedges and fallen trees blocked their path.

'Onwards to the Canal Grande! Here they stood, the proud palaces, the Palazzo Balbi and the Palazzo Contarini Del Zaffo

and the Palazzo Loredan, all mere pretence, for they were built on
the tops of a subterranean forest, and now the forest started to
move, Macbeth's marching Birnam wood. The water ham-
mered against the iron gates, it tore the boards from the joints of
the windows, it shook the gratings, a prison riot from outside.

'The sky aided the riot. The floods had not yet reached the
Merceria, but the rain had submerged it; water dripped over the
tiara and the mutilated nose of St. Alvise di Agostino, it poured
from the flower-decked balcony of the house where Goldoni was
born, it turned the smiling chapiters of the ducal palace into
weeping grimaces and Noah's beard into the limp clusters of a
forgotten vineyard.

'As the second evening approached, only black shadows slip-
ped across St Mark's Square. The street lamps no longer spread
their pink light; the water was standing so high that the circles of
light, pushed up from the ground towards the lamps, formed
large yellow blots, and were soon swept out to merge with the
others, like spreading leprosy.'

Venice, 'a labyrinth of alleys . . .'

Epilogue

Now that I have finished sifting these images of Venice, I am cataloguing the books I have collected on the journey. There's a great richness here, down to the guide and travel and illustrated books of the past hundred years, Augustus Hare's precise little volume, bound in brown with red bands and woodcuts, with judicious quotations. The dog-eared Baedeker. The 1914 edition of *A Wanderer in Venice* from the prolific pen of E. V. Lucas. Giulio Lorenzetti's proud *Historic-Artistic Guide*. Hugh Honour's civilised *Companion Guide*. James Morris' elegant discourse, with its curious erudite by-ways, and the lively *Venezia Così* by Fugagnollo. Richard de Combray's *Venice, Frail Barrier* with dark paintings by Bella is enchanting. From Reader's Digest, the lavish *Venice* is packaged as one of the Wonders of Man. The many art histories. And for pleasant browsing the following: Milton Grundy's imaginative 'anthology guide'; Ronald Shaw-Grundy's *Venice Rediscovered*; the haunting *View of Venice* from Snowdon/Hart. And the modern, scholarly appraisals by Frederic C. Lane, Brian Pullen, Philip Longworth, Peter Lauritzen, John Julius Norwich, Paul F. Grendler, John Hale; Braudel's great volumes of The Mediterranean; and above all, indispensable to start with, R. S. Pine-Coffin's *Bibliography of British and American Travel in Italy to 1860* . . .

Stray volumes – by travellers, poets, novelists, diplomats – go back into other parts of the library. But wait. Among them, is Freud's *The Interpretation of Dreams*. Freud visited Venice several times, though on the occasion mentioned in this book he forgets, perhaps unconsciously, to mention the date; and he refers to the event purposely but characteristically to talk about a dream. It must have been about 1900. He is writing about a dream of his own, a sinister sequence about ships, and fear of a warship. 'On the other hand, the analysis showed that the region of the dream-thoughts from which the warship was taken was filled with the most cheerful recollections. It was a year earlier, in Venice, and we were standing one magically beautiful day at the windows of our room on the Riva degli Schiavoni and were looking across the blue lagoon on which that day there was more movement than usual. English ships were expected and were to be given a ceremonious reception. Suddenly my wife cried out gaily as a child: "Here comes the English *warship*!" In the dream I was frightened at these same words . . .'

That is virtually all from Freud on Venice, who tended to be more lyrical, his recent biographer Ronald Clark tells me, about mountains than water. Yet surely Venice should be the psychologists' laboratory. In his generous Introduction to the 1958 Collected edition of *Eustace and Hilda*, Lord David Cecil commented that it was characteristic of the Freudian epoch in which it was written: a psychological (as well as in some Protestant way a religious) study. And to explain the Corybantic effect of Venice, a psychological as well as an aesthetic insight is needed.

The Piazza of St Mark is massed with the symbols of age, power, religion, the State and beauty: the great abstractions. There is a rich profusion of architectural styles, so many layers of Venetian history. The Byzantine, the Romanesque, the Renaissance, the Baroque and the Neo-Classical, the tactful modern. The sea is all around; to the north and west, the mountains. The vast square is framed by arches, colonnades, turrets and domes, sharp and smooth contours, making at night fantastic, fretted silhouettes. The immensely tall, arrogant Campanile was first built in the sixteenth century, a symbol of strength and both a warning and a watch-tower for enemies. It fell with a mighty crash in July 1902. 'Mrs Wolcott and I arrived at the piazza about half-an-hour after it happened and such a sight!' wrote a visitor from England (Mrs Hurst). 'Such an excitement! Such a mass of people! It all fell in a heap – tearing out the end wall of the library and destroying the loggia at its foot, but not touching the Church of St Mark of the Palace. The angel at the top fell just at the door of St Mark's. Last night we came home across the lagune and watched it for a long distance and it was so beautiful.' And it is still beautiful, rebuilt in 1912 as it was before, with the five bells called Maragona, Trottiera, Nona, Pregadi, Maleficio. The two Moors still glide out from their fastness to sound the hours from the Clock Tower, which in a confusion of imagery also displays the signs of the Zodiac and, on certain feast days, a procession of the Madonna, the three Magi and a herald. Near the water's edge, in the Piazzetta, stand the two defiant columns looted from the

The Campanile restored

East seven centuries ago, supporting the Lion of St Mark and the statue of St Theodore, symbols of the city's ancient authority. The Four Horses in bronze, taken from Byzantium in 1204, marvels of arrested grace and force, even in replica, dominate the gallery of the façade of the Basilica. They were the subject of a recent novel – half history, half thriller – by Chapman Pincher, following in a long line of popular novelists stimulated by the romance of Venice.

Will Venice disappear? Venice, in a sense, was dispersed over the centuries through acts of artistic communion that guarantee its immortality through the images it inspired. On a visit, I took a walk through the Piazza and the pigeons with Sir Ashley Clarke, who made it seem indeed like a drawing-room since he was wearing slippers and pointing out in a homely way the features he particularly cherished and the handwriting of history in every detail of marble and brick. Here was where the stallholders had driven their iron into the columns in front of the Procuratie Vecchie. There the results could be seen – on a façade of Istrian stone – of the cleaning that had been revealing past beauty before it was suddenly stopped by bureaucratic panic, in horror of the

Venice under water

The Regatta

gleaming whiteness that emerged, and fearful lest the stone would crumble without its protection of grimy deposits. (Apparently it would not, but when the decision was reversed, the money promised was no longer available – a not uncharacteristic Venetian experience.) In the palace of the Patriarch (the Basilica was the Doge's chapel; the Patriarch, kept at a distance by sovereign Venice in the old Cathedral church, was brought into the heart of the city by the Austrians), we climbed up to the little tower built high by Roncalli, the future Pope John, in order to be 'near to the angels'. But from the tower, you see the beauty of the world.

From the tower of the Patriarchal Palace, the domes, spires and lanterns of the Basilica, some shrouded for protection, seem strangely near to the touch. From just above, or at eye level, they take on a fabricated, tactile roughness and solidity. One of them looks lop-sided. You can imagine the building of them. In the distance, just sighted, is the Cathedral at Torcello, where the ancestors of the Venetians first settled. Below, stretch the thickly-packed reddish tiled roofs of the city. Under the roofs of houses, palazzi and churches are the innumerable treasures of Venice: the gold and silver, all the precious metals and gems, the mosaics and ikons and tapestries, the old furniture, books and manuscripts, the creamy marble columns, the Bellinis, Carpaccios, Titians, the dark oil paintings of Tintoretto, with their intense greens and blues, the hardware of past wars and lucrative commerce, the shops still stuffed with objects that are *veramente antichi*. All in a setting where the changing light on air and water creates magical transformations in mood and perception.

And in the year 2000 Venice will no longer exist? Its spell – intellectual, emotional, aesthetic and sensual – depends for its full potency on the fact that it is still a living city, not a ghost town, a Torcello or Tyre. Few of the impressions of Venice that I have quoted would convey their enchantment were they not seamed with the observation of the people who create the pageantry, the pride and the daily intercourse of the city. My own deeply-etched memories of Venice are of the quietness of nature and art but also of the silences broken by human activity and the human voice.

Caged birds sing in the streets. In the pulpit of a beautiful church, a plump Venetian priest astonishes you with his florid eloquence. In Montin's (where, *pace* James Morris, you can eat interestingly in Venice) the crowded tables yield the noisiest conversation in the world. In the depth of the night, the stillness is suddenly shattered by footsteps and shouts and their fading reverberation. In the morning, the bells are all at once accompanied by the chugging of a funeral barge (followed by an ambulance) as it speeds blackly along, with a gold winged ball on

Capella San Pietro: restoring the Virgin and Child

Road bridge over the lagoon   *Art Exhibition poster 1920*

the front and a gold urn astern. Take the new Burchiello to Padua from the Giardinetto of San Marco – through dismal industrial scenery, past littered banks and glorious villas – and you hear again the voices of children with the vivacity of the young Venetians on the island. In winter, the Venetians re-occupy their domain. In the Vogalunga they re-enact the Regatta and the Wedding of the Sea with dignified hilarity. But the Venetians are leaving the city in thousands every year. The population, less by fifty thousand since the early 1950s, is now under a hundred thousand.

They live in a Venice under constant threat. Though some dispute the serious danger of another flood of such force as that in 1966, the high tides – the city's only drainage system – could one day submerge the land. Various schemes have been discussed for controlling the flow of the sea through the three entrances to the lagoon.

So far, they have testified mostly to the imaginativeness of world scientists and civil engineers. Schemes for safeguarding the foundations of Venice's buildings against the gradual rise in the water level and relative subsidence of the land have been

similarly ingenious, and have proved more practical. Thus, furnished with new aqueducts, industry no longer draws on artesian
water and the water-table beneath Venice has re-established itself
very speedily. The city is no longer sinking any faster than the
surrounding land mass. Against the pollution and corrosion of
Venice through smog drifting over from the factories, and the
older depredation of saline humidity, the battle has been joined
vigorously. Chemical pollution has been reduced. An international campaign has restored many of the particular beauties of
Venetian art.

About twenty foreign and national organisations have been
engaged in restoration work, attempting to repair the neglect of
centuries of Venice's wealth of architecture, sculpture, painting.
Among them is the Venice in Peril organisation, represented in
Venice by Ashley Clarke, with zest and panache. And
UNESCO, represented with elegance by a princess from Turin.
All their efforts have been piecemeal, but impressive, indeed
visually stunning as you can see, for instance, in the case of the
pearl of Venetian churches, Sta. Maria dei Miracoli, or of S.
Nicolò dei Mendicoli, or the restoration of the Porta della Carta,
the main entrance to the Doge's Palace.

The flood opened the eyes of lovers of Venice to the extent of
the city's faded glory. But no effort so far has matched the
challenge.

In *The Death of Venice* (André Deutsch 1976) Stephen Fay and
Phillip Knightley create a 'scenario for the last days', my last
image of Venice, an anticipation of what may have happened by
the year 2000. Housing crumbles first, because of delays and
restrictions and deteriorating services. Mestre expands; Venice
shrinks. The deep canals are allowed to silt up as they did in
Torcello. The poor working class areas disappear. The palazzi are
boarded up as the rich huddle together in smaller areas. Churches
are closed. Even the best hotels, such as the Danieli, open for a
shorter season as the tourists tend to patronise the modern hotels
on the mainland. 'As the sun sets it is time to go back for an
evening meal in Mestre, or Venezia Nuova as it is known, to
distinguish it from Venezia Vecchia, or the tourist island of old
Venice . . .'

Less gloomy is the Venetian Sandro Meccoli, who sent me a
copy of his *La Battaglia per Venezia* (dedicated to his daughter

Lorenza, born in Venice) the day after I met him in Montin's. In a preface, Bruno Visentini points accusingly at the Italian State – muddle rather than malevolence – for its neglect of Venice's urgent need. In his conclusion, Sandro Meccoli affirms the truth of Visentini's proposition that the human condition of Venice is intimately linked to the 'precious and difficult equilibrium of land and water' and that the time has come for a disjunction between Venice and Mestre and Marghera, for the sake of the salvation of all three. The Italian Government's Special Law for Venice has helped arrest the decline, but is ambiguous about the future of industrial growth and hideously complicated. How can there be a true renaissance? The Italian State, argues Meccoli, is incapable of willing it or achieving it. But the will and the money for the salvation of Venice are there, internationally. The restoration, then, of an independent Serenissima? Why not? But, to be practical, Meccoli writes, let us settle for a Venice to work out its own destiny with a local government independent of the industrial zones of the mainland, and linked to the European Community.

Ashley Clarke, who introduced me to Meccoli and who has worked hard to save Venice from ruin, is quietly hopeful that the City will survive, even if the spirit of regionalism with its Chestertonian undertones is frustrated; but he commits himself only to a Browningesque 'perhaps . . .'